SO-BZF-564

Wicked PORTLAND

Wicked PORTLAND

The Wild and Lusty Underworld of a Frontier Seaport Town

FINN J.D. JOHN

Charleston · London

THE History PRESS

Published by The History Press
Charleston, SC 29403
www.historypress.net

Copyright © 2012 by Finn J.D. John
All rights reserved

Cover image: Painting of two women on front by Leland John; two little boys courtesy
Thomas Robinson of www.historicphotoarchive.net

First published 2012

Manufactured in the United States

ISBN 978.1.60949.578.7

Library of Congress CIP data applied for.

Contents

ofor.us/wpdx

Note on the QR Codes

This book is among the first nonfiction books to be published using QR ("Quick Response") codes to help bring its contents to life. A brief explanation of how they work, then, is probably in order.

What QR codes do—the reason you see them on so many advertisements these days—is automate the process of punching in a web address. Rather than bothering to find a computer and type "http://ofor.us/wpdx," you simply pull out your cellphone, open a "code reader" application and take a picture of the QR code. Up pops the web address, and all you have to do is click it and you're there.

What we're doing in this book is providing both a QR code and, for those of you who prefer not to use smartphones, a shortened version of the web address at the beginning of each chapter. It takes you to the chapter's web page, where you will find larger and usually color versions of the photos from the chapter along with other interesting tidbits, including a comments section in which you can contribute your insights.

I want to be perfectly clear here: these QR codes are for convenience, not exclusiveness. They don't take you anyplace you can't go by punching in the web address manually. This is not a "secret code" that takes you someplace only accessible to people with smartphones, like the codes in so many commercial advertisements these days.

The Wicked Portland website does not engage in data collection and marketing. It will not collect, keep, record or sell any of your personal information in any way.

If you don't have a code reader on your cellphone, I use and recommend Google Goggles, which is a free app available for both Android and iPhone phones.

Chapter 1:
A Wide-Open Frontier Town.

Page 17: The "respectable" side of Stark Street, along Third. (From *The West Shore* magazine)

Video clip: Documentary video from the U.S. GSA's Historic Buildings Series profiling Portland's Pioneer Courthouse Square, with plenty of useful background information about the origins and growth of Portland and some fabulous still photographs and period movie camera footage.

Example of the Wicked Portland website and QR code additional media.

Foreword

A s the researcher/writer/producer for the biweekly podcast series "Kick Ass Oregon History," I am always on the lookout for a riveting, stimulating and, indeed, slightly ribald tale about our beloved Beaver State. The book you are holding in your hands right now contains a veritable treasure-trove of such yarns. Be forewarned!

In Finn John's *Wicked Portland*, the City of Roses of the 1870s to 1890s bursts to life in a visceral, sensual way—though smelling more of a sultry and discounted perfume than of the brilliant and fragrant flora mentioned in our fair city's sobriquet. The reader is given a tour along the squalid but colorful streets of the North End and the businesses that defined this neighborhood—the sailors' boardinghouses, the "low groggeries" and the bawdy establishments that formed the commercial backbone of this thriving (to use the word loosely) district.

Crimps and loggers, blacklegs and prostitutes, policemen on the take and debauched legislators are all featured in this alluring book, and they are introduced to the reader in an almost friendly, familiar fashion. John ushers in both the establishment and the scoundrels (often one and the same) of our fair city's past. Figures become quite familiar to the reader, and more colorful characters could not be created by a wild-thinking novelist: Joseph "Bunco" Kelly, the shanghaier who famously justified his dealings by claiming that "sea air is good for loggers"; drunk-slinging, cigar-toking madam Mary Cook and her mythical smoke rings; Danford Balch and his murderous retaliation on the Stark Street Ferry; and my personal favorite of the historical prostitutes, "Boneyard Mary" (I dare you to find a more captivating nom de guerre).

John presents the theory that Portland was created as a "scion of New England" and became an ends-of-the-earth home for the exiled spawn of the eastern established elite. It is a reasonable hypothesis, and he demonstrates how the political machinations of these wealthy, privileged and influential select few relied on the gambling establishments and other houses of ill repute for tax income and purchased (drunken) votes. John's Portland is a dangerous place, full of opportunity and well-planned double-crosses that percolate through all levels of social standing on the banks of the sewage-filled Willamette. It is bound to be a favorite of fans of Portland's tawdry past.

Enjoy the selection in your hand, dear reader. You have chosen wisely. And I am sure that you will join me when I say I can't wait for *Wicked Portland, Vol. 2.*

—Doug Kenck-Crispin
Resident Historian, www.orhistory.com

Acknowledgements

They all sound alike, don't they, these acknowledgement sections? Well, I guess I'm not going to break much new ground on this one. I just want to thank a few people. Well, all right, actually I want to thank a LOT of people.

First, I have to thank my wife, Natalie, for sharing me with this project, helping me sharpen up my drafts and being like a one-woman focus group.

I also want to thank my father, Leland, for letting me spend weekends in a spare room in his art studio, where I was able to focus my thoughts, and for creating several wonderful oil paintings to illustrate this book.

It goes without saying (although I'm going to say it anyway) that I'm grateful to History Press editors Aubrie Koenig, Ryan Finn and Julie Foster for all their help with the process of preparing this project and for the benefit of their editorial instincts. And I'd like to thank fellow History Press author Randol B. Fletcher (*Hidden History of Civil War Oregon*) for suggesting that I contact Aubrie with the proposal for this book.

Thanks a million also to my last-minute manuscript readers—Kathleen and Chuck Koch and Pauline Conaway.

A big thank-you to the Oregon newspaper editors who have picked up my "Offbeat Oregon History" column and run with it at one time or another. I don't know all your names, but I wish I did. It's a project that has sharpened my awareness and competence as a public historian over the years. There's Helen Hollyer (and later Jeanne Olson) from the *Creswell Chronicle* and Ken

Engelman from *McKenzie River Reflections*, two of the very first to pick it up, back in '08; Becky Holm at the *Douglas County News*, whose feedback has made my whole day several times; Racheal Winter and Steve Bagwell at the *McMinnville News-Register*, who have saved me from more than one embarrassing typo; Deborah Hazen at the *Clatskanie Chief*, another sharp-eyed editor who has caught several errors for me; Jon Stinett of the *Cottage Grove Sentinel* (a wonderful small-town weekly, which it was once my privilege to edit); the always-upbeat Gini Bramlett from the *Tri-County Tribune*; Patrick Webb at the *Daily Astorian*, another early and encouraging supporter; Niki Price at *Oregon Coast Today*; Larry Roberts from the *Dead Mountain Echo* in Oakridge (the most poetic and generally awesome newspaper name in the state, if you ask me); and the editors I haven't met yet at the *Douglas County Mail*, *Coquille Valley Sentinel*, *Madras Pioneer*, *Redmond Spokesman*, *Grants Pass Daily Courier* and anyplace else that I've forgotten. Thanks also to *Corvallis Gazette-Times* publisher Mike McInally for saying yes to my first Oregon history column plan and to *Albany Democrat-Herald* editors Hasso Hering and Mike Henneke for running with it.

Thanks to fellow history writers and/or producers Bill McCash, Doug Kenck-Crispin, Andy Lindberg, Polina Olson, Randy Fletcher, Dan Haneckow, Barney Blalock, Bob Dietsche, Karl Klooster, Jeff Brekas and Melany Tupper, as well as to Scott Daniels and Rachel Randles at the Oregon Historical Society, Bruce Tabb at the University of Oregon Special Collections Reading Room, Mary at the City of Portland Archives and Ingrid at Oregon State University Archives for their help finding stuff. Also, thanks to Mark Moore at www.pdxhistory.com and Dave and Heather from www.daveknowspdx.com. I also want to thank a whole bunch of Wikipedia editors who regularly work on WikiProject Oregon, but I'm not allowed to use their real names…the handles of two are Valfontis and EncMstr.

Also, as a public historian and fan of Oregon history, I gotta thank the people at The Jack London Bar in Old Town Portland, which is like a *fin-de-siècle* Viennese salon to local-history geeks like me, and McMenamins for everything they do—preserving historic buildings, brewing great beer and being serious about the history. The Oregon history knowledge community is a fantastic bunch of people.

I must also give a shout-out to my colleagues from the University of Oregon Literary Nonfiction graduate program, class of '10. That would be Teresa Barker, Marc Dadigan, Katie Dettman, "Kona Jack" Kelly, Leslie Rutberg—and, of course, our leader, Lauren Kessler. You guys are the best.

Finally, to all my colleagues at Oregon State University who saw so little of me last term, as well as to all my students who had to wait an unusually long time to get their graded midterms back the week my images were due: Thanks, guys.

Oh, and one more thing. I'm writing this on deadline. If, in my haste to get this in, I've left you off my thank-you list, call me up and let me make it up to you by buying you lunch!

This book is dedicated to my son, Nathaniel A. John, whose enthusiasm for this project has been really heartwarming.

ofor.us/wp01

A Wide-Open Frontier Town

Jealousy and Drink Were the Causes of the Trouble.

Jones's Saloon, the well-known combination house, dance hall, fence and all-around resort, was the scene of another crime last night, of which Mamie Keckner is the victim. Mamie is fair and 30, and likewise has the reputation of being a common drunk and courtesan. About 10 days ago she was discharged from the city jail, after serving a sentence of 30 days for vagrancy.

About 10 o'clock last night she went…to Jones's Saloon, on Second and Salmon, and proceeded to tax her capacity for intoxicating liquors, and, when her husband entered the saloon an hour later in search of her, she was engaged in an intoxicated tete-a-tete with one of his deadly enemies…She was surrounded by a crowd of hangers-on about the place, who urged her to hold her ground, and she held it, but not for long.

IN A POOL OF BLOOD
About 11:15 Officer Randall entered the place and found her lying on the floor of the dance hall with her head in a pool of blood. Her right ear had been cut in twain with a knife…The officer immediately turned in a call for the patrol wagon and the woman was removed to the police station, where Dr. Weatherford dressed her wounds.

—Portland Daily Telegram, *February 22, 1893*

You wouldn't know it from looking around the Rose City today, but Portland was once a wild and somewhat dangerous place. Not too many years ago, the town that today is famous for young bearded hipsters, organic food and a thousand different kinds of beer had a very different reputation—and, dare I say, a wicked one.

This book is devoted to the "golden age of Portland wickedness," starting shortly after the Civil War and ending roughly with the turn of the new century. It's an era of free-flowing booze, open prostitution, corrupt government, crooked gambling houses and industrialized "shanghaiing." It's an era during which one police chief is a former crooked gambler accused of offering to help a convicted murderer break out of jail for a $1,000 bribe and another is rumored to have shanghaied prisoners out of the city lockup. Finally, it's an era when, every night in the old North End, gamblers and drinkers carouse and fight, fugitives lurk in clandestine opium dens and tender-footed rubes fresh off westbound trains get fleeced at faro "banks."

A WILD AND LUSTY FRONTIER TOWN

The city of Portland started as a clearing along the Willamette River, about halfway between Willamette Falls and the Columbia, established at what sea captain John Couch famously announced was the farthest upstream point to which he could bring a deep-water ship. For most of the second half of the nineteenth century, it was a rough-hewn seaport town, muddy in the winter and dusty in the summer, populated with an ever-expanding group of frontier characters: globe-trotting Yankee traders from New England; sober, hardworking midwestern pioneers fresh off the Oregon Trail; "forty-niners" from the California gold rush who'd come north to settle down; Chinese laborers fleeing from a terrible famine to work on railroads and salmon canneries in the land they nicknamed "Gold Mountain"; Scandinavian and German immigrants working deep in the woods on logging crews or manning the fleet of tiny, dangerous lumber schooners that shuttled back and forth to San Francisco; deep-water mariners from Ireland and northern England; and freshly demobilized Civil War veterans from both armies, looking to escape the ghosts of war in this most distant outpost of civilization.

Of course, bringing so many different people and cultures together led occasionally to turbulent times. The sober Quaker from Iowa, fresh off the Oregon Trail and working a small farm on the outskirts of town, had little

The Wild and Lusty Underworld of a Frontier Seaport Town

Until the Burnside Bridge was built in 1894, Stark Street—because of the ferry at its foot—was the boundary between "respectable" Portland and the North End. This drawing from 1888 shows the "respectable" side of this boundary, along Third Street. *From* The West Shore *magazine.*

The Portland waterfront as seen from the east side of the river in 1898, showing newly built sternwheelers fitting out at Willamette Iron Works. *Library of Congress.*

in common with the hard-living Confederate army veteran prospector from Kentucky, in town spending his hard-grubbed gold dust on cheap whiskey and cheaper women before riding back into the Blue Mountains to do it all again. Early Portland was no stranger to the clash of cultures.

By about 1870, Portland was still the jumping-off point, the last reasonably large town one would pass through on the way to the truly rugged forested frontier. By then, the plentiful stumps that "Stumptown" had once been known for—whitewashed so they would be easier to avoid tripping over at night—had long since rotted away, and Portland was developing a culture.

It was a city of possibilities, surrounded on every side by untapped resources: trees to cut and mill, gold and silver to mine and grain to grow in the rich black soil and export to the world through the deep-water port, as well as a seemingly unending torrent of "ever-toothsome salmon" to scoop out of the river and pack into cans.

But it was a rough place and in many ways a grossly unfair one, too—a place where you could only really expect success if you were white, fluent in correctly accented English and male. In the 1800s, Portland was no different from anywhere else in America in how it treated women; as Frances Fuller Victor pointed out in 1875, the men treated them as if they were idiots or young children.

WHO PORTLAND WAS

Writer Dean Collins told the story of Portland's creation in an essay he published ninety years ago, just a couple dozen years into the new century, at a time when Portland was still not a completely tamed town and there was still a risk of being shanghaied out of one of its speakeasies if you picked the wrong drinking companions. In it, he referred to Portland as "a synthetic city"; what he meant by this was that it had been put together using pieces of other places. Even today, ninety years later, this is still a good way to understand this ever-quirky town.

The Plutocracy: New Englanders

The initial seeds from which Portland sprouted were straight out of New England. As many Portlanders know, the town came within a coin's toss of being named Boston; Francis Pettygrove and Asa Lovejoy each wanted to name the place after their respective hometowns, and Pettygrove won the toss. But notice that neither one of them wanted to name the town Charleston or St. Louis or Chicago. This was two Yankee traders settling

A lumber crew, working with axes and "misery whips" and hauling logs out on a skid road with a team of oxen, clears land in part of what today is downtown Portland in the early 1870s. *J. Gaston*, Portland: Its History and Builders *(1911)*.

for one New England town name over another. Portland was founded as, essentially, a colony of New England.

New England is famous for its practical, conservative and hardheaded merchant class, and it's from that line that Portland's elite sprang. These were Yankee traders who came "around the horn" to Oregon on sailing ships to trade and make money, and they identified Portland as the best place to do that. They had money when they arrived, and they intended to make more. And they did.

Now, these Yankee entrepreneurs were dedicated to a real libertarian vision of trading. They seldom concerned themselves with moral quibbles when it came to business. For the most part, if you wanted to buy something, they figured that somebody was going to sell it to you and it might as well be them. So if you were planning on setting up an illegal still to sell liquor to Native Americans or perhaps a rip-roaring saloon with rigged faro games and a covey of friendly ladies upstairs, they were more than happy to rent you a building to do it in and sell you the equipment and furnishings you'd need.

Not that they were your friends, mind you. You'd have to watch yourself. Yankee traders believed in minding your own business, which meant that it wasn't their business to save you from getting taken advantage of in a bad trade—that was your job. When it came to business, they were not their brothers' keepers.

This basic libertarian-mercantilist ethic set the New England elite apart from the people from other parts of the country, chiefly the upper Mississippi Valley, who started coming in great numbers after the town was platted.

The Middle Class: Midwestern Pioneers

These midwestern folks came overland, not by sea, in covered wagons with their families inside, following the Oregon Trail from St. Louis. Most of them didn't have much money to spare. These folks were seeking not a chance to make a pile but rather an opportunity to start a new life for their families in a place with clean air and plentiful land.

Although their philosophies were different, these hardworking, sober-minded families fit in well with the Yankee plutocrats they found on arrival. Together, both of these groups of new Portlanders got busy building churches of various types and exploiting the resources—farmland, timberland, crops and trade routes—that the area had in such abundance. Portland developed for a decade or so as a town composed of roughly equal parts Boston and St. Louis, serious and hardworking and, at least nominally, god-fearing.

The Transient Classes: Sailors, Miners, Loggers and Prodigal Sons

Then came October 23, 1861, the day a man named Henry Griffin found gold in China Creek, in eastern Oregon's Powder River Valley. Gold prospecting, formerly a California and southern Oregon thing, exploded to include eastern Oregon and Idaho. Thousands of hard-living miners flocked to Oregon, bringing with them the shifty-eyed gamblers and saloonkeepers who preyed on them. When the miners hit a big strike or just decided that the winter weather in the Blue Mountains was too grim to endure, they headed to Portland, and when they got there, they expected to find someone to take their gold from them in exchange for a good time.

Also in the 1860s, Oregon's timberlands started coming to the attention of the timber operators who were getting close to the point of having cut all the commercially viable trees in the upper Midwest. Soon, vast crews of lumberjacks were camped deep in the woods, felling trees with axes and "misery whips" and living for months at a time in primitive conditions until the job was done. At that point, they'd draw their pay and bring it to the nearest big city—Portland—looking to blow it all in one great, glorious, hell-roaring binge on "the skid road" before slinking back into the woods to earn some more.

At the same time, the hard labor of the midwestern sodbusters was paying off with bumper crops of grain that needed to be exported, along with the timber coming out of the logging camps and mills. An ever-increasing number of deep-water sailing ships from places like Liverpool started calling at Portland to carry that cargo off across the sea. When they arrived, these ships were full of sailors who'd spent months on board, living in tiny bunks in a cramped and smelly forecastle, and it took a month or two to get the ballast unloaded and the cargo put in. So these sailors, several months' pay jingling in their pockets, would slip ashore to join the party.

And finally, there were the prodigal sons and remittance men. These were wealthy young reprobates from more "civilized" places—usually eighteen- to twenty-five-year-old lads who had been sent to Portland because of its reputation as a sober frontier city of hardworking, god-fearing pioneers—a pre–gold rush reputation that Portland by then no longer deserved but which it enjoyed for many years in the mid- to late 1800s and which its card sharks, bordello madams and saloon blacklegs traded profitably on for decades. These lusty lads would often get into far more trouble in Portland's North End than their hapless parents ever dreamed of them getting into back home. We'll meet one or two of these a little later in this book.

These are some rough categorizations of the sorts of young, unmarried men who, in the mid-1860s, started passing through town with money in their pockets—all collecting in the roughest and most colorful parts of town and looking for action of one kind or another.

And there really were a lot of them. Out of a population of about four thousand people in 1866, only roughly half were permanent residents. The others were what Collins calls "transients":

> *Now the incoming transient, en route to or from the gold fields [or lumber camp], had no time to make contacts with the fixed population, had he been so inclined. He craved fiercer and more stimulating entertainment than was offered in the churches or in the meetings of the Washingtonian Society.*

The traders of Portland were practical men. They had come to Portland with the intention of furnishing the people of the West with such things as they seemed to require…So they set themselves to see that the demands for new commodities should be supplied to the sweeping, transient population.

The result was that the Yankee plutocrats started figuring out a way to minister to the desires of both the "respectable" permanent residents of Portland and the hard-partying bachelor loggers, miners and sailors who brought so much money to town. And they found that so long as the two groups could be kept out of each other's daily lives, all would go on well. The New Englanders could continue profiting from trade with both groups.

For decades, they did exactly that. Portland became like two separate towns. The same laws applied to the entire town, but the difference in how they were enforced became striking. In the early years, when Portland law enforcement was still administered by a city marshal rather than an official police department, cops patrolling the neighborhoods were paid their salaries directly by the businesses and residents on their beats. If those paying customers wanted antiprostitution laws to be treated as friendly suggestions,

Couples stroll along Sixth Street in downtown Portland, in the "respectable" part of town, circa 1906, postcard image.

22

or antishanghaiing enforcement to be less than enthusiastic, the beat cops were in no position to object.

"Disreputable" Portland stayed tucked into the North End and maybe wandered out along the waterfront occasionally to stretch its legs. The growing Portland Chinatown, stretched along the river a couple streets up from the waterfront just south of the North End, provided a buffer zone, and so long as "respectable" Portlanders didn't penetrate that barrier or enter the North End, they could pretend not to notice. People from one side went years never seeing anyone from the other.

The Yankee traders carefully kept all of these groups out of one another's way as best they could and happily traded with them all.

From the outset, though, there was one big problem with this system. The wildlife of the North End kept spilling out into the rest of the town, usually by moving south into the business district. It would start with the drinking and gambling operations, which few Portlanders much minded. But then the "bad girls" would move out into the "good" part of town, and with them would come trouble.

For the most part, though, this arrangement worked beautifully for many years. Eventually, the forces of civic decency would gain the upper hand, but it would take the better part of a century, several international incidents, two world wars and, eventually, a Congressional investigation to do it.

EARLY PORTLAND GEOGRAPHY

Physically, Portland in the late 1800s was a town in which the closer you got to the river, the sketchier things became.

From up high on the west bank in what is today the Pearl District, where the lovely and stately homes of the plutocrats reposed, you descended both geographically and socioeconomically as you walked downhill toward the docks. Eventually you'd pass through the commercial district and reach Chinatown, which at that time centered on Second Street, stretched out along the river like a buffer zone between the "respectable" city and its more disreputable waterfront (the Portland Chinatown didn't move to its current location until much later). On the other side of Chinatown lay rough-and-ready First Street, as well as the warehouses and wharves lining Front Street—that is, the waterfront.

Along the riverbanks, a powerful combination of sights and smells greeted visitors. The waterfront was lined with two-story wharves, built that way so

Views looking down toward the waterfront from Second Street—then the heart of Chinatown—along Morrison and Washington Streets, in 1888. *From* The West Shore *magazine.*

that they could be used at both high and low river levels. Every year, the spring runoff brought the river levels up and damaged the bottom wharves; they were only rebuilt when absolutely necessary, so things were perpetually shabby, and there were plenty of shadows and alcoves in which to hide. The banks of the river were peppered here and there with sewage outfall pipes,

The wharves along the Portland waterfront in the late 1920s, shortly before they were destroyed and replaced with the seawall. *City of Portland Archives.*

from which evil-smelling and unhygienic substances discharged and, when the water levels were low, glopped onto exposed bits of riverbank beneath wharves and piers.

The waterfront was nearly all privately owned. The general public had little access to the river, and very few citizens had any legitimate reason to come down there, other than to pass through a narrow corridor along Stark Street, from which the ferry would bring passengers across the river to East Portland.

To the south of this corridor, the waterfront was rough enough—a watery warehouse district chiefly peopled with burly longshoremen, squirrely deep-water sailors and drunken trespassers of various sorts. To the north of the ferry corridor, the waterfront was worse. By the mid-1880s, many of its structures had been replaced with a railroad yard—which was not an improvement—and the Oregon Steam Navigation Company "boneyard" lay to the far north.

The boneyard was where old, clapped-out riverboats went to await their final dates with destiny, and some of them waited for a long time indeed. Vagrants and drifters moved into some of them, and at least one prostitute operated out of a derelict riverboat there. Few people, other than residents and customers of the prostitutes, went there for any reason, and the shadows at night were deep and long. Many secrets ended up buried in those shadows forever. Others floated to the surface after a week or two and caused uncomfortable questions and, occasionally, coroner's inquests.

PORTLAND'S NORTH END: THE "BLAZING CENTER"

Just ashore from the north end of the waterfront lay the neighborhood referred to picturesquely as the "North End." The North End covered the neighborhood that today is known as Chinatown and Old Town, almost street for street. Everything north of Stark Street and east of Park or Eighth was the North End. It was a place of sailors' boardinghouses, budget bawdyhouses, open gambling and cheap and plentiful intoxicants of every kind known to the nineteenth century. And for most of Portland's early years, it was run as if it were a completely different city from the one two blocks away from it, on the other side of Stark Street. In many respects it was.

The neighborhood was full of successful businesses of the type that are not supposed to exist but always do. For most of the century, there was an unspoken agreement that as long as those businesses stayed in the North End and preyed on sailors and lumberjacks, leaving the rest of the town free to pretend they didn't exist, they wouldn't be bothered—at least, not too much.

Portland's Municipal Rascal

Jonathan Bourne Jr.

It must have been a sunny day in 1878 when Jonathan Bourne Jr. stepped off the ship and set foot on the soil of Portland for the first time, because he immediately fell in love with the place. Portland is particularly lovable when the sun shines on it.

It had been a wild ride. Bourne had come to Portland from New Bedford, Massachusetts, by way of Hong Kong. He'd gotten into a little trouble in college, you see, back east at Harvard, and he had to drop out and sign on to a whaling ship. That had gone all right until the ship was caught in a typhoon off the coast of Formosa; the crew had just barely managed to beach it in time to get off alive, but the ship was destroyed and Bourne was once again at loose ends.

New Bedford was still too hot for him. So Bourne thought he'd try Portland instead. And now, here he was, standing on a pier in a smallish, crude frontier port city that nonetheless must have reminded him, in many ways, of New England and home.

Almost immediately upon arrival, Bourne showed himself around with the kind of raffish flair for which he would soon become famous in Portland. According to the later recollections of his friend and legislative colleague Abraham Lafferty, a few days after arriving in the town and making the acquaintance of some of the more colorful locals, he hired a cab to take a tour of his new home, "accompanied by the leading lady of a traveling show, and with an ice bucket filled with champagne bottles sitting in front of them in the cab. They drank publicly at intervals. Such was Bourne's introduction to Portland."

A fold-out poster of Portland, published in 1879. This was the Portland that greeted Jonathan Bourne Jr. when he first stepped ashore. *Library of Congress.*

And, he might have added, such also was Portland's introduction to Bourne.

Bourne was a small man, twenty-three years old, with cocky eyes that twinkled mischievously over a spectacular, fluffy moustache and "pork chops." He was carefully groomed and well dressed, witty and educated, charismatic and outgoing, rascally but not malicious—every inch the archetype of the lovable rogue.

Portland was in for a wild ride, and it would never be the same.

Over the next twenty years, Bourne would make a name for himself as the hard-living bad boy of Portland politics. And yes, he knew something about corruption; by the 1890s, he'd all but taught the Portland political establishment how it was done. Just before the turn of the century, Jonathan Bourne was as close to a political-machine boss as Portland would ever get.

As a youthful politician, Bourne perpetrated some of the most brazen and shameless acts of corruption the state has ever seen—cheerfully stuffing ballot boxes with thousands of bogus votes, arranging police protection for bordello madams and shanghai men and bribing legislators with stacks of cash, slugs of liquor and (it was rumored) the services of prostitutes. Then, as an older and wiser politician, he partnered with earnest Populist politician William U'Ren to slam the door on the whole thing by giving the voters of Oregon, for the first time, an initiative and referendum system. In the process, he may have actually been instrumental in saving much

Legendary Portland politician Jonathan Bourne Jr., as he appeared in the mid-1880s. *Oregon Historical Society.*

of Oregon's public lands by putting an early stop to the ongoing theft of millions of acres of prime timberland by a gang of sharp-elbowed out-of-state would-be timber emperors who were being ably assisted by one of Bourne's political enemies.

Most Oregonians don't know any of this. Most don't even recognize his name. Liberal progressive poets like Lincoln Steffens, who were quick to celebrate U'Ren, were suspicious of Bourne and mentioned him only minimally and reluctantly; the right-wing plutocrats whose company he once kept regarded him as a traitorous political freebooter. Only a few Oregonians today know how important this one-term progressive Republican senator was to the state.

But of course, in the 1880s, Bourne was not yet known as a progressive anything. Instead, he was known as a wild, epically mustachioed libertine and a fun-loving Falstaff, the life of every party. He also was known as the fellow who figured out what a tremendous political asset the "sin sector" of Portland could be—its seedy and dissolute waterfront, its secretive Chinatown and especially its notorious "North End." In a political system that ran on votes and money like a horse ran on hay and water, Portland's wickedest neighborhoods were a rich trove of both.

A WILD AND MISSPENT YOUTH

Jonathan Bourne Jr. was born in 1855 in New Bedford, Massachusetts—the "city that lit the world." At that time, New Bedford was quite possibly the richest town on the eastern seaboard. Kerosene had yet to be invented in the 1850s, so if you wanted to be able to see at night you had two choices for fuel to burn in your lamps: whale oil or nasty stuff that smoked and stank. Those who could afford it burned whale oil.

Young Jonathan's family could afford the good stuff. His father had gotten in on the ground floor as a whaling ship owner and, during the golden age of New Bedford whaling, became one of its biggest and most successful players. By the time "Jonnie" was a young boy, Jonathan Sr. had used his whaling profits to build Bourne Mills, a clothing manufacturer in New Bedford. This provided a nice income but lacked the romantic cachet of whaling ships, which is probably why Bourne Sr. continued to run a small fleet well after whaling's profitability had declined.

But in the days of Jonnie's early youth, whaling was still huge. It's hard for us today to fathom the deep fascination that whaling held for New Bedford kids in the 1850s. Whaling was such a profitable enterprise that every man-jack aboard a whaling ship came back from a successful cruise with plenty of cash. Ship captains got so rich that they were able to build stately hilltop

An image of ships in the Portland harbor in the 1890s, from a lantern slide. Some of these ships may actually have been whaling barques. *OSU Archives.*

homes with widow's walks on top, decorated and furnished in rich nautical style and set up high, where they could watch the ships come and go when they were in port. Skilled deckhands lived well too, and they kept families back home in respectable style. Life was good—except, of course, for the frequency with which untimely death struck. Whaling was, after all, very dangerous work.

New Bedford boys looked forward to the romance of going to sea on a whaler, and as soon as they could, many of them signed on and left.

Bourne's father obviously didn't have that in mind for his only son. Instead, the younger Bourne went off to college at Harvard. But something happened during Bourne's senior year there. Less than one year shy of graduation from what was already the most prestigious college in the country, Bourne suddenly dropped out, signed on to a ship and went off to sea.

The chronicles are silent on why he did that. But the rumor mills certainly were not. One particularly zesty rumor was mentioned in a letter to the editor of the *Portland Oregonian* from Bourne's old friend Abraham Lafferty in October 1954, several years after Bourne's death. Lafferty, while urging voters to not be so concerned about politicians' youthful indiscretions, wrote, "They said in 1906 that Jonathan Bourne Jr....had been expelled from college in Massachusetts because he hired a professional burglar to enter the college and steal the examination questions."

This apparently wasn't an isolated incident. And, according to the New Bedford correspondent for the *Boston Record*, Bourne came by his wild inclinations honestly:

> [Jonathan Bourne Sr.'s] *fondness for the society of ladies never deserted him, though he was past 70 years of age when he died. The son possessed an inheritance of something besides money. As "Johnnie" Bourne, he was known far and wide, and acquired a reputation as a "high-roller," which is not often excelled even in these days of Seeley dinners...*
>
> *Stories of the young man's exploits in Boston and elsewhere were constantly exciting the good people of this town, and were often the occasion of much breathless admiration on the part of others in Bourne's set. He acquired a reputation as an ardent admirer of the fair sex.*

"Seeley dinners" is a reference to the famously debauched bachelor party of P.T. Barnum's nephew, Herbert Seeley, which had happened the previous year. Having heard a rumor that burlesque dancer Little Egypt was scheduled to emerge naked from a giant pie, a squad of crusading policemen raided the party in the early morning hours. Little Egypt was, in fact, there, although she was not naked; charges and countersuits were filed, and various ribald details of the party ended up being unpacked in open court, much to the fascination and delight of newspaper readers nationwide.

But as for Bourne, there's surely something more that we don't know about—something big. A reputation for debauchery, expulsion from college and the threat of a misdemeanor burglary charge are significant problems, but they don't rise to the level of requiring a young fellow who is the only son of one of the richest men in town to go into exile, first on the sea and subsequently on the opposite side of the continent, for the rest of his life.

Whatever the real reason for Bourne's departure might have been, it happened in 1876 and it changed his life forever.

INTO EXILE ON A WHALING SHIP

On board a whaling ship, Bourne would have gotten a chance to rub elbows with the sailors for months at a time, fine-tuning the cross-class social skills that would help make him such a powerful force in Portland. But his career as a mariner was cut short by that shipwreck off Formosa. He survived the destruction of his ship, was rescued, made his way to Hong Kong and booked passage to the West Coast—and to Portland.

At this point, Bourne was clearly looking for a home. If he'd had any intention of returning to Massachusetts, he would have booked for San Francisco, where he could have either made his way overland or booked another voyage around the horn and back home. There was, in 1878, no train service out of Portland; the only way out was by sea or by overland stagecoach.

No, Bourne was looking for a place to stay. Essentially, he was a remittance man. As such, he was in good company. Oregon in general, and Portland in particular, was home-in-exile for several remittance men back then. Remittance men were the scions of wealthy families who were regularly being paid what amounts to a monthly blackmail payment—the remittance—in exchange for their agreement to stay far away from the family manse. Usually these were incorrigible rich kids who brought scandal after scandal down on the weary heads of their parents until, finally, they pulled some irredeemable corker and had to be sent into exile—sometimes temporarily, sometimes forever.

In 1878, Portland was barely accessible over land, and getting there by sea involved a long and dicey journey. It was about as far away from "civilization" as it was possible to get without living in a log hut and killing your own meals, and it had a population large and diverse enough to support a decent social life. It made for a great place of exile for a wealthy remittance

The clubhouse of the posh, plutocrats-only Arlington Club, as it appeared in the 1910s. Jonathan Bourne Jr. was a charter member. *City of Portland Archives.*

man who also happened to be very ambitious; he could have a great time, not embarrass anyone and perhaps even make a name for himself.

By all accounts, Bourne loved Portland right away. Here was a wide-open city, run by solid businessmen who didn't fret about petty moral issues. There were trees to cut and silver to mine. There was a thriving deep-water port. And there were places where a wealthy young swinger could have a damn good time.

And the feeling was mutual. Everyone seemed to like this young, wealthy rapscallion—rich and poor alike.

"Jonathan went through several fortunes," future governor Oswald West recalled, "and had a wonderful time doing it."

"He always dressed well," Lafferty recalled later. "He always had money, remittances from Bourne Mills...He entertained much at the best eating places and was a charming host."

Bourne was soon settled in. He became a charter member of the city's exclusive Arlington Club, the posh plutocrats-only social club that became a hallmark of Portland's upper-class New England establishment. At the same time, he was also firmly establishing his connections with the various entrepreneurs in the more "fun" parts of town.

ofor.us/wp03

Portland Saloons and Gambling Dens

FIVE SHOTS WERE FIRED

A Shooting Shindy Reported at the Crockford Saloon

Five shots fired in rapid succession startled the loungers and passers-by on Fourth and Alder streets about 10 o'clock this morning.

The shots were discharged in the barroom of the Crockford Saloon by Jess Donelson, a gambler, for the purpose of making Romeo (whose surname is unknown), a well-known sport, dance…The trouble originated in a quarrel between Romeo and Ed Nolan, another gambler, in which the latter accused Romeo of having done some very unprofessional things while pursuing his gambling operations. Romeo naturally resented this reflection on his character, and hot words were followed by blows, in which Romeo was slightly worsted. Donelson evidently had a grudge against him also, and concluded it would be very funny

TO SEE ROMEO DANCE,

so he commenced to fire off his pistol, the balls striking in dangerous proximity to Romeo's feet. At the time the shooting commenced the saloon was crowded with loungers, most of whom were gamblers, and there was a general scattering of the weak-kneed and tender-footed, who had congregated there.

A Telegram reporter was at the scene shortly after the shooting occurred, and was informed by the bartender at the Crockford…that the shooting was wholly accidental.

—Portland Evening Telegram, *Wednesday, January 18, 1893*

Front Street looking northward from Yamhill Street, with the waterfront just to the right, in 1888. One of the businesses on the left is where young J.P. Cochran started his Portland faro spree. *From* The West Shore *magazine.*

In the 1800s, Portland was a place where any cocky young rube could find a place to drink and gamble within seconds of stepping off a westbound train or inbound ship; in the mid-1870s, there was one licensed liquor outlet in Portland for every forty men, women and children in the city.

Quality was not sacrificed for quantity, either. You could get anything in one of the saloons of Portland's edgier neighborhoods—including shot, stabbed, clobbered, swindled, stupefied with opium, knocked out with chloroform, infected with syphilis, poisoned with bad moonshine or shanghaied.

Yet, ironically, Portland's reputation back east had changed little since the 1850s, when it was known as a sober, hardworking frontier town full of brave pioneers. This made it a virtual Venus flytrap for suckers from back east.

Young J.P. Cochran was one such sucker. In late November 1892, when he stepped off a passenger train from St. Louis in downtown Portland for the first time, J.P. had no idea what kind of a ride he was in for.

J.P. was the son of A.G. Cochran, general solicitor of the Missouri Pacific Railway. His wealthy father, hoping to get him away from the fast-and-loose friends he'd made in Missouri, had dispatched him to Portland and secured a job for him as a salesman for the Hammer Paint Company to keep him busy there.

The Wild and Lusty Underworld of a Frontier Seaport Town

Like many people from other parts of the country, old Mr. Cochran no doubt thought of Portland as a place full of sober pioneers, working hard and living right. Had the poor fellow had any idea what Portland was really like, he would sooner have sent the kid directly to the state pen—where he very nearly ended up anyway.

Confident and well dressed in kid gloves, patent-leather shoes and silk tie, the twenty-two-year-old checked into the plush Portland Hotel and, as the *Portland Evening Telegram*'s reporter phrased it, "immediately began to cut a wide swath."

He soon found his way down to the waterfront end of Yamhill Street, where he spent a very rewarding evening winning $1,300 in faro games. Flush with success, the dashing young champ found that in addition to having made some serious bank, he'd also acquired some new friends—"sporty professional men and capitalists of the 'short-card' tendencies," the *Telegram* reporter wrote, "who thought they would fleece the darling tenderfoot."

Poor J.P. never had a chance. In a very exciting evening at a faro bank (game) during his next visit, he pulled ahead by another $400. Then, with the baited hook securely fixed in his mouth, he went home for the night.

The next day, right on schedule, J.P. experienced a serious run of "bad luck," and his fortunes were nimbly reduced to zero. But he was still convinced that his betting strategy was a winner. After all, had it not made him $1,700 just a couple days before? If only he could get his hands on a little more money, he might yet redeem himself. After all, no streak of bad luck can last forever. (It does not seem to have occurred to J.P. that the faro dealers might have been cheating, as they unquestionably were.)

So the dashing lad went to Union Pacific Railway attorney W.W. Cotton, presented his credentials as the son of A.G. Cochran and authorized representative of Hammer Paint and convinced him to cash a draft for $250 against Hammer Paint's accounts.

Over the next few days, young J.P. wandered around town, finding businessmen willing to cash drafts for him against Hammer Paint. When this resource was fully tapped and swindled away, he pawned his watch, overcoat and silk hat. This kept him at the tables for a few more days.

Meanwhile, though, the paper that the young rake had been hanging all over town had been dishonored by Hammer Paint, which turned out to have some objections to the idea of giving its new employee an open line of credit for him to play cards with, and a detective agency was looking for him. When the agency's sleuths tracked him down, they found him sitting at a faro table at a joint on the corner of Fourth and Washington, coatless and bareheaded in the early December weather. All he had left in the world were his clothes and the fifteen dollars' worth of faro checks (chips) with which he was gambling. He was taken directly to the city jail.

About a week of iron bars and prison food later, a considerably chastened J.P. Cochran was both relieved and terrified to see his father, just off the train from St. Louis.

The elder Cochran had to do some serious smooth talking to convince the prosecuting attorney not to file criminal charges against his son; after all, the young swell had swindled three different people out of large sums of money. A.G. told District Attorney Hume an implausible shaggy-dog story about the president of Hammer Paint having been stranded on a Caribbean island, unable to apprise his company that Cochran was authorized to gamble with the company's money.

"I am convinced my son had no idea of swindling anyone, because he supposed his drafts would be honored," Cochran told the *Telegram* reporter afterward, presumably with a straight face and good eye contact. "This is the first time my son has ever gotten into trouble. He is only a boy of 22 years, and his generosity always keeps him close-run for money. He has been well raised, has an excellent home, and has never wanted for anything; but this gambling mania has done all this for him."

District Attorney Hume finally agreed to drop the charges. Whether he did that because he actually bought the Cochrans' story is impossible to say for sure—although he later mentioned the case as an example of a situation in which a young, impetuous person ought to be given a second chance, so it's a pretty good bet that he did not.

"I am not at all sorry that he was arrested," the elder Cochran told the *Telegram* reporter as the two were leaving the county jailhouse, eager to get on an eastbound train and shake the dust of Portland from their feet. "In fact, I rejoice that he was put in jail, where I had a notion of permitting him to remain for a while longer. He has been taught a severe lesson, and a good one."

"Yes I have, Father, and I shall profit by it too," the younger man offered contritely.

Young J.P. Cochran and his father were soon safely aboard a passenger train, heading back toward St. Louis, both eager to leave behind the wild and lusty frontier city whose character they'd both misjudged, each in his own way. It's pretty unlikely that either one ever set foot in Portland again.

Over the years, a lot of money flowed from young tenderfoots like J.P. Cochran across green felt-covered tables and polished mahogany bars downtown. And not all their stories ended as happily as J.P.'s.

And then there were the variety theaters. These bore very little resemblance to the tonier Broadway-type theaters such as the New Market. Essentially, they were saloons with low-budget theatrical productions going on, in which the actresses would come out after the show and vamp the guests, persuading them to buy champagne and drink with them (the ladies keeping their heads by pouring their drinks discreetly into spittoons while their customers got more and more sozzled and free with their spending). You might think of these joints as the ancestors of modern strip clubs.

These institutions caused more wailing and gnashing of teeth in "respectable" parts of Portland than the regular saloons and the bawdyhouses combined, mainly because people saw them as an open and welcoming gateway into perdition, as noted here in the December 28, 1892 *Portland Daily Telegram*:

To the Editor—

What revenue does the city derive from the so-called variety theaters? True, they pay a retail liquor license—but don't all saloons pay that? Do they pay anything extra for enticing men and boys into boxes, there to be plied with vile liquor by a lot of brazen harlots called song-and-dance artists, and there robbed? The price they charge for their vile alcoholic stuff is 25 cents per drink, when first-class saloons only charge 10 cents and 12½ cents for good liquors, as such beverages go…

How many heinous crimes can be traced direct to these variety theaters? How many boys and young men take their first downward step while crazed by the liquor dealt out by these leeches? How many unmentionable acts are done while their perpetrators are under the spell of passions awakened by scenes witnessed on the stages of these places, in which scantily attired males and females participate?

—A Parent

Opium Dens

Portland's Chinatown stretched along Second Avenue, centering on Alder Street, and as the nineteenth century wore on, it grew until it formed a sort of buffer between the commercial district and the waterfront. There were saloons in Chinatown, too, along with Chinese lotteries, fan tan and other gambling games, prostitution and everything else—but in that district, the drug of choice was opium.

In the more "respectable" parts of town, Chinatown and its opium chilled the blood. Stories of warren-like passages between buildings, through thick oak and iron doors and secret passages activated with a hidden latch, as well as a veil of secrecy and silence behind which unspeakable acts were committed by implacable and sinister "celestials," were the ripe stuff of hair-raising stories in pulp magazines well into the 1940s.

The reality, though, was a lot less romantic. In Chinatown lived a population of mostly bachelors who had come to Oregon to make money but hadn't earned enough to get home to China. They were stuck, and by the 1890s, they'd been hounded out of other major towns by armed mobs; if they were secretive and silent, it's because they didn't want to give anybody an excuse to get the torches and pitchforks out again. And if they did, the byzantine tunnels facilitated escape in worst-case scenarios.

Fugitives from justice with friends in Chinatown often found those opium dens handy places to hide out from the law. But for the most part, they were refuges for Chinese laborers looking for a taste of oblivion, so they could forget for a while that they were marooned in a strange land far from their families.

Most other Portlanders, though, didn't understand this at all. The tone of this excerpt from the *Portland Evening Telegram* on November 29, 1892, is a good example of what they had to face:

It Was Not Suicide

A Greatly Excited Husband Who Thought His Wife Had Taken a Poisonous Dose

A Confirmed Slave to Opium

Early this morning an excited Chinaman rushed into the coroner's new office and begged Coroner Holman to do something for his wife, who was dying from the effects of a dose of poison…

As the woman had not yet reached the stage where his professional services were needed, the coroner sent word to the police station, and City Physician C.H. Wheeler was hastily summoned…and found that it was only a hysterical fit…

On ascertaining that the woman was a white person, although married to the Chinaman, a Telegram reporter repaired to the scene to investigate the matter. Being informed that they lived in a brick building on Yamhill Street, the next door to Cordray's Theater, he made his way thither, and found the building a veritable nest of Chinamen. Up a flight of dark, rickety stairs he ascended, while the air was permeated with reeking and stinking odors. After wandering around among the innumerable labyrinths of dark alleys, he ran on to a crowd of Chinamen huddled together in a dirty, slimy box-like apartment, sickening with the fumes of opium and that peculiar nauseating odor of a Chinaman.

Questioning them as to the whereabouts of the "sick woman" only brought a blank, stolid look into their idiotic faces, and it was not until after the reporter had gone through a pantomimic exhibition worthy of the powers of Salvani that a ray of intelligence shot across the faces of the Chinamen.

They directed him to…[where] on the bed was a woman reclining, while near her was a tray containing an opium pipe, pills and lamps…

The woman told a rambling tale of how she was married a year ago to her present lord and master, Tom Loui. They were happy, she said, very happy. She had all the opium she wanted, and until a month ago, had smoked constantly. Then she had tried to quit, and she thought her abstinence was the cause of her late hysterics…

A lad 13 years of age came in, and she pointed to him as her son. Evidently she had been married before. Dr. Wheeler will call the attention of the Humane Society to this case, and will probably have him placed in the care of that society…

The reporter sighed. Surely it made no difference to him. He thoughtfully wended his way out of the gloomy building—and the woman went on smoking…

GAMBLING IN PORTLAND

In late 1800s Portland, most saloons that were not variety theaters were by definition gambling dens, and the saloonkeepers who ran them were gamblers by trade. When a young man like J.P. Cochran stepped up to one of their tables, he was seldom playing in an honest game.

That was especially true if he was playing faro. Faro was the most popular gambling game of the nineteenth century, but it died out completely early in the twentieth when gambling fell under stricter regulation. The reason? For the house, faro only makes sense economically if you cheat. An honest faro game offers such a slim "house edge" that it's simply impossible—and economically dangerous—to offer one. And because faro was played with a special dealing box, there were dozens of virtually undetectable ways to cheat.

In fact, by the 1890s, every faro game in every saloon in the country was dirty—with a tiny handful of special-case exceptions. The only

Spectators watch a faro game in 1910 in Reno, Nevada. *Library of Congress.*

"square" faro games being played were private games among friends. If a saloonkeeper had a faro game going in his place, it was a cinch that somebody was cheating somebody.

One such saloonkeeper was Edouard Chambreau, a French Canadian gambler, fighter and all-around blackguard who, after he converted to fervent cold-water Christianity, wrote an extensive, articulate and brutally frank memoir of his early life. He intended it as a sort of confession, as well as an example to other sinners—the idea being that if a man as wicked as he had been could be saved, so could they.

Chambreau's story shows him to be an unusual man, but the saloons he ran were not much different from the other six dozen sprinkled around Portland in the late 1800s.

Edouard Chambreau, Saloonkeeper and Gambler

Edouard Chambreau—whose name might have originally been Charbonneau, although he was probably no relation to the more well-known Jean-Baptiste

Charbonneau, Sacagawea's son—was born in France in 1821 and came to Montreal with his family in 1825. He became a tailor's apprentice in the late '30s but hated it, and in 1838, at age seventeen, he left home and spent the following few years traveling around Canada and the United States with various blackface minstrel shows and, once, a circus. This is where he learned the trade that he would later ply in Portland—gambling, setting up rigged games of chance and plying suckers with liquor—and started making a real study of the methods of winning in fair games and fleecing players in foul ones.

Edouard Chambreau as a young man. *Leland John.*

He found his way to Oregon in 1847 and was in a Vancouver prison when word of the California gold rush reached Oregon the following year. With the help of some friends, he broke out of jail and ran to San Francisco to join the rush.

Chambreau seems to have had no thought of going out into the country to look for gold; his plan was to let others do that and take it from them afterward.

In the Gold Fields with Portland's Future Police Chief

In San Francisco, running with his usual rough crowd, Chambreau barely got out of town with his life after he helped start what amounted to a gang war.

It seems that he and one other strapping young lad from a circle of toughs who called themselves The Hounds had gotten into an exchange of gunfire with some Mexican miners. (Remember, California had been part of Mexico just a few months before this.) In the ensuing fracas, the other Hound, Jim Beatty, was shot and killed.

The Hounds responded to this affront by perpetrating a massacre on the Mexican and Chilean mining camps. Dozens were gunned down, killed and wounded, their belongings smashed or looted and their tents burned. (Chambreau does not say whether he participated in this massacre or not.)

It was too much. San Francisco sat shocked for a day or so and then gathered itself together with an implacable and vengeful fury. Vigilante groups sprang into existence. Mobs of armed and angry men started fanning out over the city looking for Hounds. Chambreau disguised himself as a tramp and stowed away aboard a schooner, whose first mate he bribed to help him get out of town.

Stockton, the town to which he fled, wasn't much more receptive, and he barely escaped being lynched there after being caught harboring a robbery suspect.

After that, Chambreau spent a few years drifting through mining camps and towns, essentially as a professional gambler. He had several additional scrapes with angry mobs, particularly the sorts of mobs that form after a local has been fleeced in a suspicious card game and shots have been fired or knives used.

In about 1850, he visited his old friend James Lappeus, a onetime fellow soldier who probably had also been one of the Hounds, who had settled down a bit and was now operating a saloon, gambling house and general store called Ten Mile House just north of Sacramento. He arrived just in time to help Lappeus defend his business from a large, drunken cohort of teamsters that had started a big brawl in the store. Chambreau and Lappeus drove them out by throwing bottles at them, but once outside, they started shooting into the store.

"In an instant we both had our six-shooters out, and you think it was not lively there for a little while?" Chambreau wrote. "After we had driven them away from near the store we retreated, and barricaded ourselves inside, and made ready for an attack, but they did not want any more of it. We were both hurt but nothing serious."

You may have recognized Lappeus's name; he would later become Portland's city marshal for several years and later served for fourteen years as its chief of police. When Chambreau later wrote that "any desperado who had the necessary abilities could always be elected City Marshal," he may well have been thinking of Lappeus.

A portrait of James Lappeus, the former gold field gambler who became Portland's city marshal and, later, its chief of police. *Leland John.*

Both Lappeus and Chambreau were in Portland just a few years later, and both were running saloons. Lappeus settled down there in the brand-new, stump-strewn city, but Chambreau soon left again for the new hard-rock gold fields of Idaho.

But 1867 found him back in Portland again, running a crooked saloon and gambling den.

SALOON KEEPING IN PORTLAND

It wasn't as if Chambreau didn't try to straighten out, at least a little. His first business in Portland when he came back was a restaurant. The problem was that people would eat a hearty meal and then refuse to pay. This cost Chambreau a lot of money, but not for the reason you might think. It wasn't the cost of the lost food that hurt. It was the legal costs associated with thrashing the deadbeats, something it does not seem to have occurred to him to stop doing.

"I had already paid three fines for 'firing' men out because they would not pay for what they eat, until one day a tight one by the name of Buckskin Bill came in, called for a good meal, and when he got done eating, he said he would pay me another time," Chambreau wrote. "Well, I used this man up so bad he had to be taken off the sidewalk in a cart. The fine was $90" (the equivalent of $1,700 today).

Perhaps this was because the restaurant was in such a bad part of town. It was right next to a "free and easy dance house" and a saloon-gambling hall in the North End. Eventually, Chambreau sold his restaurant and went into partnership with the owners of that saloon and dance house, going back into the liquor trade, despite his wife's pleas.

When he wrote his memoir several years later, Chambreau clearly felt that this new saloon was the moral low point of his liquor-mongering career.

A view of the North End under water during the flood of 1894. This image was taken from First and Stark Streets, looking northward toward Burnside. *City of Portland Archives.*

"This was one of those places where 'everything went,'" he wrote. "This place was open for everything that talked, from the highest to the lowest of both sexes. Any one could be accommodated with fun, amusements and games of all kinds with cards or other devices."

The only record we have to go on here is Chambreau's own account, so it's impossible to say for sure if he was implying that his business partners—a man he identifies only as "Sam R" and a woman he never names at all—were brokering or engaging in prostitution. But he sure makes it sound that way. And he does mention that there were "girls" working there, whose business was fleecing suckers in some way—if not as prostitutes then probably as variety-theater dancers.

Chambreau wasn't long involved with this particular "hell-hole." It's a good bet that the fact that women were involved made it particularly tough for him to sell the whole idea to his wife. He spent a year or two as a freelance gambler, opened a liquor store, lost it in a fire, opened another saloon and lost it in another fire and opened a third saloon—all this in the space of three years.

Finally, in 1874, he gave up the business and became a serious, earnest Christian temperance man.

A TYPICAL PORTLAND SALOON

So what exactly did this liquor business entail in an early Portland saloon? Well, that really depended on what kind of joint you were running.

But a saloon in Portland in 1873 was, almost without exception, a place you went to gamble. It might be a low-stakes poker game among friends at a convenient table or in a private room that the average customer didn't know existed or it might be a formal setup with a faro dealer pulling cards out of a specially built dealing box. But it was always there.

Not every saloon cheated the gamblers who came. Plenty of them stuck with selling liquor and let their customers gamble if they wanted to, with no house involvement—a good example being world-famous logger joint Erickson's Saloon at Second and Burnside.

But many did cheat, and Chambreau's was one of them. His contrite memoirs are a priceless trove of details about how he and his fellow blackleg saloonkeepers did this. There were a number of ways.

Often the saloonkeeper would have employees or associates participating in games, keeping the pot boiling. There were poker players at outlying tables

The Gem Saloon and the Oro Fino Saloon and Theater, located on First Street between Oak and Stark, as they appeared in 1876. The Oro Fino was Portland's largest and most prestigious theater until the New Market Theater was built. It was half owned by James Lappeus, who at the time this image was made was serving as Portland's chief of police. *Oregon Historical Society.*

participating in what looked like informal, ad hoc games, who pretended not to be associated with the bar in any way but were secretly on the payroll and using sophisticated methods to cheat. Then there were "cappers," players in the house games who looked and acted like regular customers but were in on the scam and who would win several hands and make it look like the house was paying out. They'd play with decks of cards that had been marked in subtle ways or modified with a card trimmer or with decks that were missing a key card or two.

"When the cappers would bring in a man or 'steer a man,' I would deal myself," Chambreau wrote. "If it was 'short cards,' I would take a hand. If it was any one that had to be caught or beat at the counter, I always had ten different dead [rigged] games that I could put my hand upon behind the bar."

"Short cards," by the way, means a game in which the dealer has pulled a couple key cards out of the deck to improve the house's odds. Also, if Chambreau was doing the dealing, chances were pretty good that the game wasn't on the level. He'd actually invented a little machine that he wore on his wrist, just up his sleeve, that would silently shoot three preloaded cards into his hand as he cut the deck. This gadget had been invented to overcome the home field advantage when Chambreau was gambling in other operators' saloons, but he surely deployed it a few times in his own shop as well—along with all the customary things like rigged faro dealing boxes, marked or wedge-cut cards and weighted dice.

"FIXING THE POLICEMAN"

A smart saloon operator made sure that he was on good terms with the local law enforcement community, especially if he was running one of the less respectable houses. In his memoir, Chambreau gives some priceless descriptions of how those connections helped in one of his North End saloons—the one he helped operate after closing his ill-fated restaurant:

> *Among the first things I did when I took charge of this hell hole was to fix the policeman on my beat. Now, every candid man knows there is a vast difference between a restaurant and one of those abominable places. Still, I was better protected by the police in the hell hole than I was in the restaurant.*

Chambreau goes on to give a few pointers on how to manage an angry, freshly fleeced sucker, with the help of a friendly constabulary:

> *It was not everyone who lost money at the games, or who the girls beat, that would squeal. Some would have too much pride and honor to be known to have been in one of those places…But there are another class of men, and I think the very ones who ought to be "beat." That kind will only bet on a "sure thing." This kind, in my opinion, ought to be thrown down very hard. Now, I will tell you how it was done when any of those cases were reported to the Chief of Police* [Lappeus]. *The Chief in all probability would send a policeman with this victim, who knew already all about the case, and who also would be a friend of mine, and who knew right where to find me. They could come to the saloon and inquire for the guilty parties. This would be during the day when there are few people in. They would make some inquiries, the policeman would say, "I will give any man $100 who will tell me where so-and-so is," and the bystanders would not know but what this was on the square.*
>
> *Finally, the policeman would tell this poor man to meet him at a certain place, while he would* [investigate another angle]. *He would then lose no*

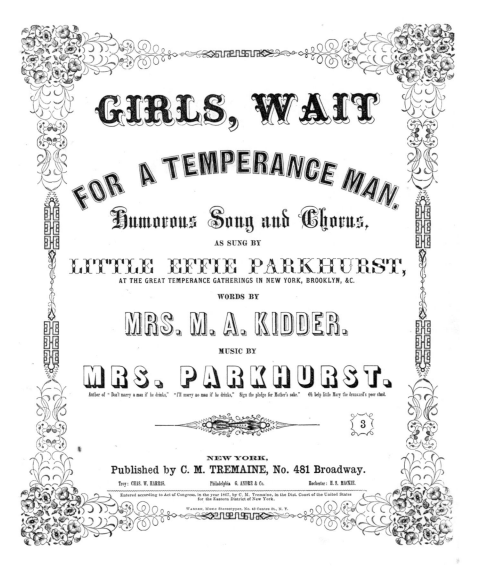

The front cover of a booklet of sheet music for a song written in 1867 to be played and sung at temperance rallies. *University of Oregon Special Collections.*

time in coming direct to me; then the bargain would be made. I usually gave one-third to the policeman, but it was always settled according to how much trouble was made about it…He would then go direct to the Chief. What took place between them the public has often made good guesses about.

> *He* [the policeman] *would then return to this poor man, and he would tell him that he was on the track of him, but that it would take some time as the gambler has gone to San Francisco or Idaho, or somewhere else. The policeman would tell him to go home, that as soon as he caught this man or this woman that beat him out of his money, he would write to him...*
>
> *If the man made considerable trouble, and had lost much money, and he would not be put off that easy, and was liable to bring it before the grand jurors, then he would be bought off; but this was seldom the case, because the officer would tell him the parties who swindled him out of his money were not responsible for nothing.*
>
> *Let me tell the reader that there is not one case in a hundred that ever comes to trial. Men who usually lose money in such places are, as a general thing, strangers which cannot afford to wait, and the officer will take advantage of this and put him off until the man gets disgusted and leaves town.*

By the spring of 1874, Chambreau had left some of that deviousness behind him. His new saloon, while still not on the level, was subtle enough to not require the regular interventions of a friendly police chief.

That's the year when the great Portland temperance crusade was launched, and upper-class Victorian ladies in their Sunday best started coming around pestering him to let them come in the saloon and sing and pray. It was their efforts that finally inspired him to quit the business and go straight.

ADVICE FOR THE YOUNG

Chambreau's autobiography ends with a lengthy appendix in which he gives the full details of how to cheat at pretty much every gambling game known to nineteenth-century Portland. Starting with the ever-popular faro, he goes methodically through them: Rondo, Keno, High for Luck, Lansquenet, Crib, Draw Poker, Bragg, Monte, Black and Red, Chuck Luck, dice games, Euchre (which he spells "Youker"), Seven-Up, Twenty-One, Three-Card Monte, Cut or Trimmed, Roulette, Wheel of Fortune, The Locks, Peruvian Snuff Box, the Strap Game, The Thimbles, Telegraphs, Propes, Three Cards from the Top and something called "The Coin Swindle."

At the end of this lengthy education in the applied science of separating fools from gold, Chambreau offers some advice for those who might be thinking longingly and romantically about a life as a roving gambler or saloon blackleg. It's worth looking over, if nothing else as an antidote to the Hollywood vision of how these fellows lived. And it boils down to a simple, heartfelt "Don't do it!"

I will use every effort and every means in my power, and if I succeed in turning one young man from going that way I will be thankful to God and consider myself more than compensated for my labor.

Besides being very expert in all these [techniques]*, you ought to be a number-one fighter. This* [is] *because it is very necessary ofttimes to persuade your opponent that you are right, and that the money is yours; in fact, it is claimed that you have to kill at least one man before you can be anybody.*

To every 1000 young men that start out to be a gambler, 999 will fail. The first 300, their health will not permit it; 200 will go to the penitentiary; 200 drunkards; 25 will commit suicide; 75 will be hanged; 100 will get killed; 100 will not amount to anything. The community classify that class [the last 100] *as gamblers, but it is a mistake. Some don't pretend to do anything but live off of prostitutes; some beg their living, and cheat everyone that will trust them for anything.*

ofor.us/wp04

North End Girls

Accourding to the fellows who'd seen it, Nancy Boggs's bordello was something else—Nile green and crimson, rising two stories off the deck of an old sawdust barge floating at anchor in the middle of the Willamette River in the early 1880s.

Nancy was a brothel operator in early Portland. Hers was a profession that was just barely illegal at the time—prostitution had been outlawed in Portland in 1871, but in the North End, this was more of a suggestion than anything. In fact, although it sometimes put on a good show, Portland's city government seemed to go out of its way to avoid effectively enforcing antiprostitution laws.

One of the reasons this was the case was because of liquor taxes. It's always been pretty easy to tax things that society frowns on, like liquor and tobacco. The people who participate will buy them anyway, and the people who don't participate feel it's okay to tax these things because people really shouldn't be using them. One couldn't levy a tax on sex, of course, but the bordellos served a whole lot of liquor too. So did the variety theaters.

The three city governments—Portland, East Portland and Albina, which would one day unite to become a single city but had not gotten around to doing so yet—taxed liquor by the drink pretty heavily, and they'd come to depend on money forked over by the sinners of Portland to pay basic expenses. For instance, Portland in 1880 got a full one-third of its revenue from liquor taxes. If the brothels got shut down, a significant percentage of this revenue would go away.

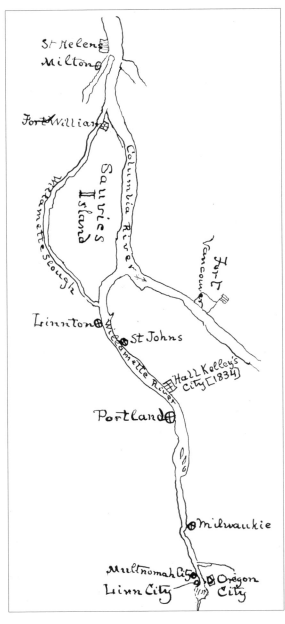

A hand-drawn map from the 1860s of what today is the
Portland Metropolitan Area, showing the location of
Portland's various early competitors for regional dominance.
J. Gaston, Portland: Its History and Builders *(1911).*

Like any small business owner, Nancy chafed at the heavy hand of the tax man. But unlike the other North End madams, Nancy had figured out how to dodge it: her "whisky scow." It was 40 feet wide and 80 feet long, which gave the bordello she had built on it a relatively small footprint, a mere 2,500 square feet or so. She doubled that by making it a two-story building. Legendary Oregon writer Stewart Holbrook—who got the story from an old waterfront character named Edward "Spider" Johnson, a former Erickson's Saloon bartender with whom he bent an occasional elbow in the 1920s—described Nancy's floating palace this way: "The first floor was devoted entirely to Baccus; the second, to Venus."

The beauty of the scheme was that it dramatically expanded the market for Nancy and her girls. On each side of the river, hired guys in rowboats would pick up customers and ferry them out to the brothel. Once there, a customer would find a plethora of tax-free goods and services at his disposal.

It wasn't a perfect solution. Liberal applications of alcohol have a nasty tendency to make people think that they're better swimmers than they actually are, and at many times of year the current at mid-Willamette is faster than anyone can swim. For the most part, if a guy jumped or fell off the barge, he was a goner. And this happened with some regularity.

Something else happened with some regularity, too: police raids. Remember, both Portland and East Portland thought that Nancy's palace was their heifer to milk. As they saw it, taxes and other municipal benefits were being stolen from them, and they couldn't be expected to sit idly by.

And here's where the brilliance of Nancy's scheme really shone through. First off, she had a big list of satisfied customers on both sides of the river, some of them cops, and they kept her well connected to the rumor network. Every time one of the two cities ginned up a police raiding party, somebody tipped Nancy off, and she'd simply weigh anchor and, with the help of a mariner friend (she had lots of those too, a fact that will be even more important later in this story), get her little floating island of iniquity towed to the opposite shore. Though each city claimed jurisdiction over the river, Portland could not exactly claim to own the waters lapping at the shores of East Portland, though it might have liked to. Back would go the raiding flatfoots to report the failure of their mission—no doubt with a convincing show of regret.

On those occasions when East Portland put together a raiding party, she'd do the opposite, and the visiting police would find her facilities tied off to a wharf on the west side. The police would make a grand show of going out in force to bring her in, only to be "foiled" again.

This worked great for a year or two. The two cities, although they got along well in public, were most definitely rivals in the struggle for power and influence on the river, and not only that, each of them claimed jurisdiction over Nancy. Neither one was about to help its neighbor collect the taxes that were rightfully due to itself.

Still, they had to keep trying. As you've probably gathered, it's quite likely that the cops were just going through the motions at the behest of higher-ups at city hall so that nobody could accuse them of not doing anything.

Things changed, though, in the early 1880s. Remember, the unwritten rule in Portland was that anything goes as long as it doesn't leave the North End. Well, the middle of the Willamette River was not the North End. On a clear day, passengers on the Stark Street Ferry—at the time, the main way to get between Portland and East Portland—would have been able to see people frolicking on the barge. It's easy enough to imagine that your city

The stern-wheeler *Wide West*, built in Portland in 1877, shown sometime before it was dismantled ten years later. It is possible, albeit very unlikely, that the *Wide West* was the boat that participated in the midnight rescue of Nancy Boggs's floating bordello in 1882. *Salem Public Library.*

is clean, virtuous and vice-free if all the naughtiness is tucked away into a corner of town that none of your neighbors regularly visit; it's a lot harder if, every time you cross the river, you pass a giant, raucous, Christmas-colored reminder that it's not.

In 1882, the citizens of Portland were angry enough about the apparent unwillingness of their cops to crack down on vice that they started putting pressure on the city and the police to do something. So, in the spring of that year, the cities of Portland and East Portland got together and arranged for a joint sting operation on the floating barge.

Now, here's where this gets suspicious. Nancy's friends on both police forces surely told her what was going on. Why did she not move on down the river to Albina for a few days? Could it be that the dramatic events that followed weren't entirely spontaneous? Were the cops staging a grand performance for the benefit of their respective city halls? The historical record of this episode isn't very complete, so we don't know. But even today, 120 years later, through the lens of Spider Johnson's waterfront folklore, the story still has the distinct aura of show business.

Screaming and cursing, Nancy fended off the cops' boats with a hose, blasting scalding steam from the brothel's heating plant, which she just happened to have all rigged up and ready to go. This must have looked and sounded pretty spectacular from shore, and best of all, scalding steam drops in temperature pretty quickly in damp, chilly spring air, so the chances of anybody actually getting hurt would have been pretty low. Naturally, though, in the face of such fierce resistance, the cops broke off quickly and started pulling for their respective shores again.

But that evening, under cover of darkness, somebody—nobody knows who, but it was almost certainly not one of the cops—paddled stealthily out to Nancy's barge and escalated the situation with a sharp knife, which he used to cut the bordello's anchor line.

Now, just in case your familiarity with the Willamette River consists primarily of standing on the seawall in west Portland and smiling down on the families playing happily on its placid surface, I should let you in on a little secret: the Willamette is a much more fearsome river than it looks from far away. Its currents are smooth but swift, and this is especially true when the water is high, as it was at that time. Once liberated from its anchor, Nancy's place went downstream fast, heading toward Swan Island and, eventually, Astoria and points west—that is, the open sea. Something had to be done and quick.

Nancy probably realized what was happening when the line was first cut; the boat would have lurched a bit as it transitioned from being stationary to traveling north at about three miles an hour. In any case, she figured it out soon enough.

Although a successful professional businesswoman in what you might call a fairly liberated line of work, Nancy was, after all, a Victorian-age woman. Like most women of her time, her first instinct was to seek help from a man. But this wasn't an option on this particular night. The only man still on board was a customer who'd hit the jug particularly hard and was passed out upstairs, sleeping it off. This character was exactly as helpful as you would expect a guy like that to be. So Nancy let him sleep and went to get a rowboat.

With a word of encouragement to her girls—who must have been fairly freaked out at this point—she started pulling strongly for the east side of the river and the "neutral" city of Albina.

Once ashore at Albina, she rousted a riverboat captain she knew—never mind how—and explained the situation to him.

The skipper didn't need a picture drawn for him. As soon as he learned that a barge full of girls and whiskey was floating down the river, in mortal peril and in need of rescue, he leaped into action. It seems pretty likely that his crew wasn't too hard to motivate either. They had the boiler warmed up in a trice, and not long after that, the sternwheeler was thrashing its way down the river in hot pursuit of the damsels in distress.

A view of the grain docks at Albina in 1888, as seen from the water. *From* The West Shore *magazine*.

When the sun came up the next morning, Nancy's little island of iniquity was once again riding peacefully at anchor, a few miles downriver at Linnton.

Precisely what arrangement Nancy and her girls made with the captain and crew of the sternwheeler to thank them for their gallant midnight rescue is, happily, lost to history. The name of the sternwheeler and skipper both are also lost to history. Chances are good that, if the steamboat company had found out, the captain would have been disciplined for doing it; it costs rather a lot of money to fire up a steamboat and run around the river all night on it.

Nancy and her forces had won the day. But they must have known that it was a fight they couldn't win in the long run. Soon afterward, then, she brought her operation ashore in the North End, setting up shop in a regular land-based place on Pine Street near the waterfront and sending her first liquor-tax payment in to the city hall there.

Nancy's houseboat may have come ashore as well, ending up in an entirely different location. There's a bed-and-breakfast in Portland today that, local legend has it, was the structure Nancy had built atop the sawdust barge. Removed from its footings, it supposedly was transported a few blocks away from the river and set up on a foundation as an ordinary house. You can

A crowd gathers at First and Stark Streets to celebrate the completion of the Northern Pacific Railroad line in 1883. Nancy Boggs's new on-land bordello would have been located two blocks to the right of where the photographer was standing to make this picture. *Salem Public Library.*

book a room in it today, and it's just possible that you're spending the night in a room once occupied by one of Nancy's mariner girls. It's called the Fulton House Bed and Breakfast.

PORTLAND: THE "WIDE-OPEN CITY"

The story of Nancy Boggs's maritime misadventures is one of the better-known stories of early Portland prostitution.

The historians of early Portland don't talk much about the girls, and it seems none of the girls themselves bothered—or dared—to write their stories down for themselves. What we know about the entrepreneuses of frontier Portland is almost all filtered through a few key sources, all of them men. Chief among them is "Spider" Johnson, the old waterfront character who filled Stewart Holbrook's ears with this and other folkloric, mostly true stories of scarlet sisters, shanghai artists and crimps.

We do know that for a while there was almost an entire block of "cribs"—little rooms just big enough for a bed, a washbasin and a window seat at which available girls would sit leaning on cushions and looking coquettishly through the window at male passersby—on Yamhill Street around Third or Fourth, deep in the "respectable" part of town, which historian Malcolm Clark calls "the court of death." This caused all sorts of trouble, because the churches were just a few blocks uphill from them; it was particularly a problem after one of the girls there, Emma Merlottin, was hacked to death with a hatchet by an unknown assassin in 1885 in one of the most high-profile unsolved murder mysteries of 1800s Portland.

Luckily, one of the financial pillars of the community stepped in to help. The story is, he bought a big building deep in the North End and made it available to the ladies, who happily moved. Their benefactor got a guaranteed high occupancy rate on his income-producing property; the girls got a location much more convenient for purposes of enticing freshly paid sailors and lumbermen; and mainstream Portland got to get back to pretending that their city was relatively vice-free. Everybody won.

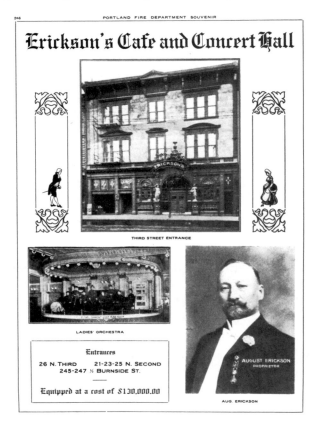

An advertising flyer produced by famous North End loggers' watering hole Erickson's Saloon in the late 1890s. Edward "Spider" Johnson worked at Erickson's as a bartender.

Everybody, that is, except the ones who considered antiprostitution laws to be more than a friendly suggestion. But then, for years, they more or less were. The 1880 census lists a total of 58 prostitutes in Portland. However, it also lists 247 "seamstresses." That would be about 1 seamstress for every 85 men, women and children in Portland. It seems like a pretty safe bet that more than a few of those seamstresses were augmenting their sewing income in other ways.

ELIZA "BONEYARD MARY" BUNETS

One early Portland businesswoman whom it would be really nice to know more about was Eliza Bunets, a forty-year-old character who was better known as "Boneyard Mary." As her name suggests, Boneyard Mary lived in the steamboat company boneyard, probably on board one of the derelict steamboats. In the city directory, she listed her occupation as "laundress," and, well, maybe she was.

Boneyard Mary would likely have gone unnoticed to history if she had not been involved with a sort of love triangle that ended in a suspicious death in the boneyard in 1878. Moreover, looking over the evidence today, it looks pretty clear that she was more than just a witness.

The story begins with the mysterious disappearance of a longshoreman named William McMahon on February 10, 1878. McMahon was in charge of a scow moored in the river and lived aboard, not far from where Boneyard Mary lived. As neighbors, the two knew each other, although it is impossible to say how well; there's no record that suggests that they had any kind of intimate relationship, but if they did, that would explain a few things.

On this particular evening, McMahon's friend W.H. Harrigan was out drinking with him, and McMahon was clearly afraid of something. He asked Harrigan if he'd come to the boat with him for the night. He was worried about a man, Jack Abrahagen, who was in jail for beating and knifing him a few days earlier; he thought Abrahagen might be keen to finish the job so that he wouldn't be able to testify against him in court later. Why McMahon was so worried about Abrahagen when he was still in jail isn't clear; perhaps he thought Jack might have some well-armed friends. Perhaps he was right.

Harrigan told him he'd come spend the night with him on the scow, but he was relieved of the need to do that when McMahon was arrested later that night and chucked in the city drunk tank. And that was the last Harrigan saw of him alive.

61

The notorious Oregon Steam Navigation boneyard, where the steamboat company parked its old and dilapidated steamboats, as it appeared in 1892, long after Boneyard Mary had moved on. *Portland City Archives.*

Harrigan came to check on him the next day and found no sign of him anywhere. Knowing that he must be around, he beat on the scow's cabin door and finally kicked it in. McMahon had vanished, leaving all his things behind, including, most alarmingly, $4.50 in cash.

"I then started for up town," Harrigan told the court at the subsequent coroner's inquest, "and as I passed the house of Boneyard Mary, she called to me and said McMahon had fallen in the river, and she saw him swimming; but she thought he had got out as someone struck a light in the scow." She also volunteered that "Mac" had gone to Washington to get away from Abrahagen, he added.

Harrigan must have thought it odd and suspicious that Boneyard Mary would flag him down just to tell him this, apropos of nothing. Clearly fearing the worst, he came back with grappling irons to try and fish around for McMahon's body, although he found nothing. However, a few days later, a boy fishing off an abandoned steamboat hooked and reeled in the unfortunate McMahon's corpse.

Boneyard Mary told the coroner that "Mac" had passed her place very drunk that night, and she'd heard a splash and saw him in the river. She did not raise any kind of alarm over the man in the drink, despite the fact that a ship was anchored right next to the scow and its crew would have been in a great position to help him get out of the water. But she did go ashore to alert some neighbors that he might need help, and when they came back to check on him, they'd found a wet hat on board the boat—meaning that he must have climbed back aboard.

It's hard to imagine how that wet hat—the presence of which the neighbors confirmed—could have gotten aboard the boat unless somebody planted it there. And it's also hard to fathom how McMahon could have been coming home "very drunk" and falling in the river the night he was thrown in the drunk tank. Typically, drunks weren't released from the jail until after they were mostly sober. It's even harder to imagine a very drunk man, soaking wet from falling in the river in February, deciding after climbing out that he needs to leave immediately for Washington Territory—without even stopping to change out of his wet clothes or grab his money.

In any case, Boneyard Mary and the neighbors decided that McMahon must have fled to avoid having to deal with Abrahagen and thought no more of it until Harrigan arrived—so she told the court.

Harrigan was right to be suspicious. Eliza "Boneyard Mary" Bunets wasn't exactly a disinterested witness. At the inquest, she told the coroner that she thought the fight between Abrahagen and McMahon had broken out over her—that "Mac" had said some uncharitable things about her and Abrahagen had risen to her defense. Abrahagen, it seems, had been living with Boneyard Mary for several months, and she had been visiting him in jail and smuggling letters to him—and they were engaged to be married. So she had a motivation to stop McMahon from making trouble with Abrahagen, one way or another.

Moreover, Bunets was forty years old. At that age, in 1878, a woman couldn't look forward to many more years of work as a "laundress." Should something happen to ruin her chances to become "respectable" again, she would be left with nothing. With her entire future at stake, it's hard to overlook the powerful motive Boneyard Mary had for wanting McMahon out of the picture.

So, what really happened here? Well, a competent prosecuting attorney might offer the jury the following hypothetical scenario.

After the fight, Boneyard Mary realizes that if McMahon testifies in court against him, Abrahagen will likely go to the state prison for attempted murder, probably for some years, which will interfere with her plan to become a respectable married woman again. So she decides to rub him out. Maybe it's her idea, or maybe it's suggested by Abrahagen—remember, they're smuggling secret letters back and forth at the jail.

After McMahon is released from the drunk tank and returns home, Boneyard Mary comes over to his place with a bottle and a smile. She vamps him a bit. They drink together, and she slips a little something into his glass. A few minutes later, he's unconscious, and she's quietly slipping him over the side and into the cold, muddy river, where he sinks out of sight. Then, needing a friendly witness or two just in case, she dips his hat in the river and plants it on the boat, then goes up to the neighbors' place.

"Help!" she shrieks. "Mac fell in the river! Help me rescue him!" They come down and witness the wet hat but no sign of McMahon. Where could he have gone?

"Oh, that's right!" Boneyard Mary exclaims. "He was talking about going to the Washington Territory. Maybe he went there!" The three of them talk it over and decide that, yes, he must have gone to Washington.

Of course, it's 1878, and the West Coast is sparsely populated. Washington isn't even a state yet, and Seattle is barely more than a lumber camp. There are still bears and hostile Native Americans around. If McMahon runs away to Washington and never returns, no one will even notice, much less suspect Boneyard Mary. And it's February; the Willamette River is rushing to sea. If the body does wash ashore, it'll probably do so someplace where nobody will recognize it. It's the perfect crime…until that dratted meddling kid catches the corpse with his fishing pole.

Could this be what happened? Possibly. But we'll never know, because the coroner ruled it an accident, and everyone moved on. As for Bunets and Abrahagen, they both disappeared into the mists of history; Bunets is in the 1878 city directory ("East side Front Street foot of Flanders"—that is, the boneyard), but neither of them is listed in 1879 or later.

Liverpool Liz and Her "Senators"

Elizabeth "Liverpool Liz" Smith was a British girl who ran a joint called the Senate Saloon. Beyond pouring drinks, of course, Liz's staff offered a variety of other goods and services as well. But to keep up a respectable appearance, she called her place the Senate Saloon, apparently to differentiate it from the other Senate down in Salem, which on occasion wasn't much different.

Liz's most devoted constituents were not politicians but sailors. At that time, a lot of sailors were from England, and most of those were from Liverpool. Liz's brothel was like home for these guys.

On top of that, Liz herself was possibly the only person in the whole North End you could trust with an envelope full of cash. She had a huge safe behind the bar, and the sailors and loggers who didn't want to get rolled and robbed—or who just wanted to be able to get drunk and play poker without waking up having gambled it all away—would leave their cash with her. Sure, they'd probably end up blowing most of it at her place anyway, but presumably they knew they'd at least get their money's worth.

She wasn't above pulling a fast one on the occasional sucker, though. Spider Johnson told Holbrook that at times when there were only four or five guys in the place, some out-of-town big spender would sometimes swagger up to the bar and order a round for the house. It was the work of an instant for Liz to ring a remote bell—there was no electricity at the time, of course, so it was probably a hidden bell cord. This would alert any girls upstairs who weren't otherwise engaged to come flocking down the stairs calling out drink orders (for champagne, of course). The poor sucker who'd anticipated dropping a dollar or two setting up five or ten drinks suddenly found himself picking up a ten-dollar tab.

Liz was known as an excellent businesswoman, but she did make one particularly bad business decision: she got into bicycles. In the 1890s, bicycles were something of a craze nationwide, with people riding them all over the place. The "safety bicycle"—the basic design still used today—had just been invented a few years before, all but eliminating the danger of sudden and grisly death that was the major drawback of the old high-wheel "ordinary bicycles" of the 1880s, especially when going down a hill. (Picture what happens when you hit a bump and pitch forward over the front of that huge wheel.)

Safety bicycles also opened the sport up to women—with the old high-wheel bikes, in addition to their dangerousness, any woman crazy enough to try riding one would quickly find her skirts tangled in the spokes and probably also offer a most unladylike view to anyone standing in front of her. The safety changed all that.

Liz bought a bicycle track, put a saloon in the middle of it (of course) and outfitted a number of her employees with "wheels" along with brilliantly colored riding costumes with scandalously slit skirts. Then she sent them out all over town in search of business.

This seems to have had an unanticipated but perfectly logical effect: suddenly the more respectable Portland women became extraordinarily loath to go out on bicycles, and this more or less shut down the entire bicycle craze, leaving Liz with a lot of money invested in real estate and inventory.

Cordray's Musee Theatre, a popular vaudeville house in downtown Portland, as seen in the late 1880s. *From* The West Shore *magazine*.

Eventually, the Senate Saloon faded away. By a few years into the twentieth century, there just weren't enough deep-water sailors to keep it busy anymore.

MARY COOK AND THE IVY GREEN

Mary Cook ran a colorful combination brothel-saloon known as the Ivy Green. As Spider Johnson described her to Holbrook, she was a powerful Amazonian type, six feet tall, with a penchant for large cigars and a gift for blowing smoke rings. Reportedly, if a customer held out a finger, she'd blow three smoke rings around it.

Mary ran a respectable whorehouse, and no disruptiveness was tolerated there. Holbrook wrote of a particular day in 1896 when an amateur prizefighter named John P. Sullivan came into her bar. John P. was no relation, so far as I've been able to learn, to contemporary professional pugilist John L. Sullivan, nor to famous Portland shanghai artist Larry Sullivan—although Larry was also an amateur pug.

John P. quietly soaked up a couple tumblers of flammable spirits and then stood up and threw down the glove: "I can lick any sonuvabitch in this place," he announced, looking around the ample crowd for takers.

He found one.

A few minutes later, he was skidding to a stop on the board sidewalk outside the Ivy Green. Mary had secured him by the scruff of the collar and the seat of the pants and slung him out the door, professional bouncer style. It took her two tosses to get him across the floor and out the door, and when he picked himself up, he was covered with splinters of wood—remember, there always were plenty of loggers in town, and two-by-eight planks get pretty splintery after a couple thousand loggers walk across them in corks (caulked boots—then as now the standard logging boot, with steel spikes sticking out of the soles for maximum traction on slippery logs).

"I hated to do it," she said afterward, according to Holbrook, "but I just gotta keep my refectory a decent place for gentlemen."

THE OPEN DOOR AND THE GREAT VICE CRUSADE OF '96

On a rainy evening in December 1885, some people walking by Emma Merlottin's little house at Third and Yamhill heard screams and rushed to investigate. There they found Emma, mangled and lifeless, the fresh victim of an axe murderer who'd just managed to get away.

Emma was, as the *Portland Evening Telegram* phrased it, a French-born "nymph du pave" well known around town. Born Anna DeCoz, she was thirty-three years old. And as scarlet sisters go, she was fairly high in the hierarchy. Plenty of people who were not customers knew her socially. Rumors started swirling that the murderer had been someone important—a successful businessman. This may very well have been true. No one was ever arrested or even publicly identified as a suspect.

Be that as it may, the event got the good people of Portland thinking about the plight of the poor "fallen woman" and the "life of shame" she was compelled to lead. Churches started talking about creating a home for "wayward girls and fallen women," a refuge for the reformed prostitute in which she would no longer have to, as they saw it, sell her virtue to buy her bread.

It took ten years, but in 1896, such a place was finally built and ready. It was called the Open Door—a really rather unfortunate choice of names, but a nice idea nonetheless.

The Open Door was established in a building in the North End, near Burnside Street at 25 Northwest Fifth. The committee considered, but turned down, an offer by major North End property owner Richard Williams to supply a building free of charge. The members suspected Williams's motives in making this generous offer, possibly for reasons related to the provenance of Williams's nickname—he was known around town as "Slippery Dick."

The hat was passed around the city to various retail businesses, which responded generously with donations of furnishings, hardware, kitchen equipment and telephone service. Soon, under the watchful eye of house matron Mrs. Lucy Morgan, the place was ready for boarders.

Meanwhile, the police department had its part to do, and it was doing a yeoman's job—if, perhaps, a little reluctantly—at the urging of the newly elected reform-minded mayor, William Mason. Horse-drawn paddy wagons rumbled over the cobblestones from joint to joint, packing freshly arrested ladies of the evening into the city jail to be arraigned before the court. Bail was set at $100 each.

So, how did the girls fare in court? Rather well, actually. An example would be the proprietress of the number-two bordello in town, Miss Della Burris. Della ran a sumptuous palace for her courtesans and their paramours, located on Park Street between Alder and Morrison—just a few doors down from some of the city's most influential churches. She numbered as clients some of the most well-connected men in town, and among the top-shelf whorehouses of Portland, her place yielded only to that of Madame Lida Fanshaw. And yet, even she was arrested, loaded into a paddy wagon and trucked down to the city jail, where she remained for just a few minutes.

Miss Della promptly pleaded "not guilty" to the charge, which was "Operating a Bawdy House." She paid her $100 bail and went home to wait for her trial date. When it came up, she appeared in court, and the trial judge had this to say before summarily dismissing the charges, according to Holbrook: "Common fame and general reputation are not sufficient evidence to convict anyone of keeping a bawdy house. The positive fact of lewdness…must be established beyond all reasonable doubt."

Which was, of course, perfectly true. But wait. The cops arrested her without gathering any evidence beyond "common fame and general reputation"?

So it appeared. And it was not an isolated incident.

The Wild and Lusty Underworld of a Frontier Seaport Town

Madame Fanshaw, by far the most highly regarded of all the city's "scarlet sisters," was also carted off to the hoosegow, along with all twelve of her employees. Brought before the court, her case was not dismissed, but it didn't have to be—the jury found her "not guilty." Likewise acquitted were all her girls, and back they went to their sumptuous palace of sin at 151 Seventh Street (now Broadway), just across the street from the Arlington Club.

Well, sure, you might say. Madame Fanshaw was even more well connected than Della Burris. After all, it was at her place where the son of one of Portland's top plutocrats, walking in, was startled to meet his father walking out (this according to Holbrook, who carefully avoided mentioning any names). Her guest register, if read aloud in the Episcopal church, would have emptied the place out. Surely, like Della, she just had to pull some strings, right?

Perhaps. But that doesn't explain why the conviction record for less influential ladies of the evening was no better. There's a record of North End girl Ida Bell, of 104 Northwest Fourth Street, having been acquitted after telling the court that she was a laundress, not a prostitute. The court, having been presented with no actual evidence to the contrary, sent her forth to continue soaking her customers and/or their clothes.

And down the line they went. Rich and poor, high-class and low-rent, it didn't matter. They arrived in court, they pleaded innocent, they were found not guilty and they were back working hard for the money within minutes—because no evidence had been gathered to support a conviction.

It appeared that the police—who knew from professional experience what kind of evidence is needed to secure a conviction—were simply rounding up suspects for the district attorney to throw charges at in court, where a speedy acquittal awaited them so long as they weren't dumb enough to plead guilty. Again, the scent of show business still hangs heavy on the air, twelve decades later.

The *Portland Morning Oregonian*, for one, was not fooled, and in an editorial on April 10, 1895, it called the whole swindle out:

> *This is the net result of the moral crusade: Twenty gamblers were arrested and indicted. Two have been acquitted, and the rest will be, "for lack of evidence." The same number of prostitutes were arrested, and about half the cases so far considered have resulted in indictments…Then 12 Chinese gamblers were arrested and indicted, but not yet tried.*
>
> *The District Attorney gets $5 for every arrest; $7.50 for trial; and $15 for convictions. In each case, having taken pains to draw all the indictments separately, if there are no convictions, he will make from $500 to $600.*

The police justices and constables make about $12 out of each case, or as much more, and the county foots the bill. This is the total visible profit of the moral crusade so far—about $1,200 diverted from the pockets of taxpayers to those of officials.

Meanwhile, in the Home for Wayward Girls

However, for the forces of civic decency and moral virtue, there was good news coming from the Open Door, the newly established "home for wayward girls and fallen women" up in the North End. Ineffective as it was in court, the increased law enforcement pressure seemed to be having the desired effect on Portland's bad girls. The Open Door started to fill up as ladies of the evening checked in and put away their makeup. As April wore on into May and June, they poured steadily into the Open Door. By early July, it was chock-full of the "wayward" and the "fallen."

Then the logging camps shut down for the midsummer break, and the North End was deluged with strapping lads smelling of pitch and whiskey, with four months' pay jingling in their pockets. And then a funny thing started happening. The girls at the Open Door started going out to grab a few supplies at the grocery store and not coming back.

As it turned out, the reason the Open Door had been so popular was that its opening had been perfectly timed to get the girls through the tough early summer season, when there wasn't much business because the loggers were all in the field. Now that the boys were back in town, it was time to go out there and get some money from them.

By the Fourth of July, House Matron Mrs. Lucy Morgan was once again alone in the Open Door, listening to the distant sounds of hell-roaring in the nearby logger joints. By the end of the summer, the reformers had given up on the whole thing.

ofor.us/wp05

America's Most Pernicious Shanghai City

Mr. Chairman, I will state that there is one port on the Pacific Coast that has always been known as the greatest crimping [shanghaiing] *den in America. I refer to the port of Portland.*
—*Andrew Furuseth, president, International Seamen's Union, in testimony before Congress in 1911*

In October 1891, a twenty-one-year-old farmer named Aquilla Ernest Clark arrived in the big city to see the sights and maybe show himself a good time down around the "blazing center" of the North End—Second and Burnside.

Almost immediately, he met up with a friendly stranger who introduced himself as Smith. Upon finding out that Clark didn't have plans for a place to stay, Mr. Smith suggested a sailors' boardinghouse on the corner of Second and Glisan, where he could stay for free.

The boardinghouse seemed like a friendly place, full of picturesque deep-water sailors smoking pipes and listening to accordion music. None of them were drunk; everything was fairly orderly. Clark relaxed and settled in for the night.

The next morning, newfound friend Smith offered to buy breakfast for Clark and eight other fellows at the house. Over the meal, he mentioned that a friend of his named Larry Sullivan was putting on a party—he'd rented a steamboat for a journey down to Astoria and back. Would any of them care to join the throng?

A scene in the Portland harbor, circa 1899, postcard image.

Clark didn't need to be asked twice, and neither did the other eight guys. Soon the nine of them were waiting by the dock for the ninety-foot steamboat *Iralda* to arrive to take them all on their daylong adventure. It looked like it was going to be a great one, too—a group of fine-looking young women soon arrived for the event as well.

On board the riverboat, the party got started right away; by this time it was probably about 9:30 a.m. Smith immediately stood a round of drinks—whiskey and a cocktail known as a "peach blow," the signature drink of one of the tonier Portland hotels. There was a band on board, and the girls—with a most unladylike forwardness, at least by Edwardian-era standards—promptly started grabbing partners for dances. Awkward and young, the breakfast group sought the smooth self-assuredness that comes at the bottom of a tumbler of whiskey, and soon everyone was having a great time.

At about 1:00 p.m., the guests of the mysterious Mr. Sullivan were treated to a sumptuous lunch featuring steak, oysters, crab and salmon, along with plenty of whatever distilled spirits they might want and four kinds of wine. By the time they all got to Astoria, Clark and his new breakfast friends were very tipsy indeed, and nobody disagreed that this Larry Sullivan guy sure knew how to throw a great party. No one seemed to notice that they hadn't met him yet.

The four-masted 2,300-ton barque *Arracan*, one of the last of the British grain fleet, at the wharf in Portland below the Broadway Bridge in about 1913. *Salem Public Library.*

When they arrived at Astoria, Mr. Smith pulled out a sheet of paper. They were all going ashore to see the town, he explained, and he didn't want to risk leaving somebody behind. "We'll have an hour ashore and then we'll go back to Portland," he noted to the sozzled sightseers. "Just to make sure all of you are on board when we leave, sign your names on this passenger list. Then when we are ready to go, we'll make sure that everyone is here."

The young fellows signed the list, eager to get ashore and continue the day's festivities. Presumably the girls did not; perhaps they stayed on the riverboat—the story isn't entirely clear on that point. But soon the men from the boardinghouse were ashore, barhopping and seeing the sights at Oregon's number-two seaport city.

Then Smith innocently asked if anyone might like to go check out a real, live, deep-water ship. Enthusiastically, they agreed, and Clark led the throng, leaping into the boat that was taking them out into Astoria Harbor for a tour of the barque *T.F. Oakes.*

Once they were all on board, guns came out. The "passenger list" they'd all signed when they were too tipsy to bother to read had not been a passenger list at all—it had been the ship's articles. By signing it, Clark had changed careers. He was a farm boy no more, and he would not see Portland again for seven years.

He was a sailor now. Like hundreds of others in 1890s Portland, he'd been shanghaied.

SHANGHAIED IN STUMPTOWN

Next time you're having a nice quiet pint at Kelly's Olympian, the White Eagle Saloon, Dan and Louis's Oyster Bar or some other historic pub near the waterfront in Portland, take a look around. The place you're relaxing in was, not too long ago, the world's most dangerous place to go out drinking.

The danger wasn't so much that you might end up getting mugged or knifed, though. The real risk in 1890s Portland was that you would wake up on the foredeck of a barque, fifty miles offshore, with a violent and sadistic first mate kicking you in the ribs and yelling at you to get up and get to work. The last thing you would have remembered would likely have been a friendly stranger who chatted you up at the bar and maybe even bought you a drink.

You see, Portland was a port town with a real waterfront human-resources problem: there was plenty of work doing something other than being a sailor. And that made sailors hard to come by. Here's why:

If you were a twenty-year-old man in 1890 with no family to take care of, and you didn't mind working very hard under primitive and dangerous conditions, two opportunities were available to you:

You could go into the woods with a logging crew. It was dangerous work—many loggers of the day were missing fingers, toes and limbs and had gone to a few funerals for colleagues crushed to death by logs. Logging camps were no paradise, but the food was okay and there was plenty of it; the pay was okay, and there was no place to spend it; and if at any time you decided you'd had enough, you could quit and draw your pay.

Your other option was to sign on to a sailing barque and become a sailor. It was even more dangerous—most sailors of the day had been through at least one experience in which they seriously believed they were about to die, and all knew at least one who had died at sea. The food was horrible, and there often wasn't enough of it. The pay was okay, but advances against it could be drawn without your permission by boardinghouse operators and clothing merchants claiming to have sold you things.

Sound good so far? Wait—there's more. The ship's officers had blanket permission to beat you, imprison you and dock your pay. If one of them got a little too enthusiastic while beating you with a belaying pin and killed you, it was considered an accident. And if you ever decided that you'd had enough and quit, you would not be drawing your pay. Not only did you forfeit any wages you were owed, but you'd also probably be jailed as a deserter. That's because once you signed on to a ship, you were an indentured servant—a piece of chattel for the duration of the voyage, like a cask or a belaying pin. Walking off the job was tantamount to theft; you were somebody else's property.

To kind of put the cherry on top, merchant mariners in the 1890s were widely considered the dregs of society. The life of a sailor had once been thought of as somewhat romantic—a devil-may-care profession in which you never knew which day might be your last, a sort of perpetual state of war against the sea, a job for the kind of James Dean bad boy that young women have always found appealing. Well, by the 1890s, that was all gone. The status of sailors had been in steady decline for years, and at the end, it had reached the point where many people thought of them as subhuman. They were looked down on by every other class except hobos and Chinese laborers, to whom they were generally considered equivalent in social standing.

Sailors' social status was so low that in 1897 the U.S. Supreme Court actually ruled that the Thirteenth Amendment protection against involuntary servitude—slavery—didn't apply to them and that sailors categorically did not merit the full rights of citizenship.

So, again imagining you're that twenty-year-old unattached male, why would you voluntarily choose to sign on for a voyage to Hong Kong aboard a ship that might sink in a storm, whose officers had blanket permission to beat you, imprison you and cheat you, to live on a diet of wormy hardtack and brackish water, with no personal dignity and no control over where you'd go or when you'd return—and for less money than you could make working equally hard setting chokers on a logging operation and wolfing down pancakes and coffee every morning?

You wouldn't, of course. And so it was that the merchant marine fleet of the day found itself with a serious labor shortage in Portland.

Of course, there would have been a simple market-based solution for this simple market-based problem: just pay the sailors more money, right? I'll pause a moment so you can finish laughing and catch your breath. Right, so that wasn't an option. How else could deep-water ships acquire crews but through systematic kidnapping?

CRIMPING AND SHANGHAIING

In the 1800s, when a sailing ship ready to leave a seaport found itself short a few crew members, its captain always knew where to turn. He'd find one of the specialized boardinghouses designed for sailors—squalid and unhygienic hole-in-the-walls tucked deep in the roughest and cheapest area of the waterfront. The characters who owned these boardinghouses called themselves "boarding masters"; everyone else called them "crimps," after the Dutch word *krimp*, which was a holding tank or pen for live fish, like the aquarium full of live lobsters at some seafood restaurants. You can see the analogy here: sailors would be held there, ready to serve up whenever a customer might come in and order one.

Crimps were the most scurrilous operators in a waterfront business community that was itself one of the most scurrilous in the world.

Third Street in Portland, looking northward, postcard image dated 1907.

The Wild and Lusty Underworld of a Frontier Seaport Town

Here's how the crimps operated under normal market conditions—that is, when there was not an acute shortage of sailors. A sailing ship would come into port, making for the wharf. "Runners" for the crimp's boardinghouse would row out in Whitehall skiffs to meet the ship, clamber aboard, pass out bottles and invite the sailors to come stay at the crimp's place "on credit." This was not usually a tough sell; it would leave more of the sailor's pay free for him to spend having a good time drinking and whoring—like loggers, sailors were, on the whole, less keen on gambling than you might think they'd have been.

After moving in, the sailor would have a fantastic time until the money ran out, which it always eventually would; no sailor ever willingly went back to sea until the money was gone and he was starting to get hungry. At that point, even if he'd resisted the blandishments of the crimps at first, he was more or less forced to check into a sailors' boardinghouse, where he would be put up and fed and an account kept.

Eventually, a ship would need a crew, and its captain would contact the crimp. The crimp would walk over to the sailor and clap him on the back. "John, the *Sea Witch* needs a crew, and it's time for you to go to sea," he'd say.

"Oh, I can't go now," the sailor would say. "I'll walk right down and sign on to the next ship, but I'm not ready to go back to sea yet. And isn't the *Sea Witch* old Bully Waterman's ship? I want nothing to do with him."

"Ah, well, that's all right then," the crimp would say. "We'll sign you on to the next one. Come have a drink with me."

Most boardinghouses had a house bar with bottles of special liquor in stock. A couple swigs later, the sailor would wake up on the foredeck of the *Sea Witch*, having been delivered unconscious, wrapped in a tarp, the night before. When he woke up, he might very well find that he'd been charged for that last doped drink as well, just to add insult to injury.

Eventually, some sailors got wise to the "let's have a drink" routine, and the crimp would have to get creative. When all else failed, crimps were not above marching sailors down to the wharf at gunpoint to sign them on. If the sailor was unconscious, the crimp would forge his name on the ship's articles; nobody ever bothered to check.

In addition, a bill, signed by the sailor or forged by the crimp, would be presented to the skipper for the unpaid boardinghouse rent, with a request that it be paid off as an advance against the sailor's wages, and the skipper, having no particular dog in the fight, would usually pay off, no questions asked.

Other vendors did the same thing—clothiers were particularly notorious for selling the same suit of clothes to a dozen or more sailors, each of whom had his new threads abstracted from his sea-bag and replaced with a worn overcoat and perhaps a moth-eaten sweater stripped off a corpse before burial. Author Dillon tells of one sailor who found the comfortable peacoat he'd bought replaced with a formal swallowtail coat apparently stolen from or discarded by a wealthy plutocrat. Aquilla Ernest Clark, the farm boy who went on Larry Sullivan's party boat, ended up with sixty dollars deducted from his wages for the party—a good three months' pay for a sailor—and he had to leave most of the rest of his pay behind when he jumped ship in Le Havre. It took him seven years to get back home to Oregon.

For his services in supplying the sailor, the crimp would receive a bonus of $30 to $90, depending on market conditions. This bonus was popularly referred to as "blood money." In Portland, blood money bonuses got as high as $120 at one point, driven to that jaw-dropping level by collusion among the boardinghouse operators. In San Francisco during the gold rush, the blood money bonuses were even higher than that, and crimps—who weren't exactly morally upstanding citizens to start with—developed a wide range of new tricks to earn these jackpots. These new tricks were what became known as "shanghaiing."

THE ART OF THE SHANGHAI

Shanghaiing involved leaving the boardinghouse behind and prowling the town, looking for strangers who might be rendered unconscious, dressed up like ABs ("able-bodied mariner") and cashed in on the foredeck of a sailing ship.

Shanghaiing was done on an ad hoc basis. Sailors were shanghaied out of taverns, where naïve strangers could be chatted up and drugged. They were shanghaied out of whorehouses, where female accomplices made business arrangements with men and then, in the privacy of their "cribs" while consummating the deal, knocked them out with chloroform. When all else failed, they were shanghaied off quiet, dark streets with a blackjack and a tarp.

None of these tricks was started in San Francisco or Portland. But it was in those two cities where they became an industry, a tradition and a legend. Even the term "to shanghai" got started on the West Coast, because that was the port for which many of the deep-water ships out of Portland and San Francisco were bound.

As time went by, shanghaiing in San Francisco started to fade. By the mid-1890s, it was Portland's turn, and by the turn of the century, Portland was widely acknowledged as the most pernicious shanghaiing port in the world. It actually generated international incidents with the governments of France and Great Britain—although these governments were clearly more motivated by the captains' complaints of the growing expensiveness of crimping than any sincere humanitarian concerns for their sailors.

BUNCO KELLY, THE BUGSY SIEGEL OF PORTLAND SHANGHAI GUYS

Joseph "Bunco" Kelly was a short, burly, affable man with a large moustache, originally from Dublin (some sources say Liverpool, but contemporary newspaper stories disagree). He'd gone to sea (voluntarily, apparently) at a young age and, at some point, found himself in the harbor at Portland. For whatever reason, he decided that this was the place for him, and so he deserted, came ashore and started his illustrious career as a crimp with a particular flair for the art of the shanghai. His career was to be a colorful one—too colorful for his own good, as we shall shortly see.

He wasn't all that successful as a general-purpose crimp, running a boardinghouse and all that—although from time to time he tried. No, Bunco was a shanghaiing specialist, and nobody else quite had his panache. He is reputed to have been fond of saying that sea air was good for loggers. Bunco, by the way, was very likely the mysterious Mr. Smith from the story of Aquilla Ernest Clark.

Bunco got his name by pulling a particularly brazen stunt one day: he stole a six-foot-tall wooden Indian from a cigar store, wrapped it in a tarp and cashed it in for fifty dollars in blood money—or so the story goes. (Like most stories of Portland crimping, this story comes from Spider Johnson via Stewart Holbrook. Solid academic sources on this subject are hard to find, as you can imagine, so much of what we know of the Portland shanghai scene is tinged with folklore.)

Notorious shanghai artist Joseph "Bunco" Kelly as drawn by a newspaper staff artist during his 1894 murder trial. *From the* Portland Evening Telegram.

A view looking north on First Street from its intersection with Morrison Street. The Snug Harbor Saloon and Johnson & Sons Undertaking Parlor were about one block to the left. *From* The West Shore *magazine.*

The Wild and Lusty Underworld of a Frontier Seaport Town

There's another Spider Johnson story about Bunco that's considerably more egregious, not to mention horrifying. It also might be completely false—and if it is, that would be interesting, because it's by far the most well-known story of the old Portland shanghaiing scene. Here's how it goes.

It seems that one night Bunco was on the prowl for ABs to fill a big order he'd received at a time when the Mariner's Rest, the boardinghouse he sometimes kept on Second Street, was empty. He was down to prowling the waterfront in search of strangers to clobber or, um, drink with. Bunco had a special proprietary knockout-drug concoction in tablet form that he called "Kelly's Comforters," which he'd used with some success to drug unsuspecting plowboys, loggers and miners, and presumably he was packing a few of these with him now. But on the way to the Snug Harbor Saloon on the corner of Second and Morrison, he came upon an open cellar door. Wafting out of it was an odor that was strangely familiar, but he couldn't quite place it.

Holbrook's account continues:

> "In those days," Bunco Kelly later told Spider Johnson, who in turn told me, "in those days, I always carried a small dark lantern under my coat. I got it out and lighted it, and threw a beam below. I couldn't see nothing but the little ladder disappearing into the darkness."
>
> Bunco was game, however, and he went slowly down into what he described as the damnedest reek he ever hoped to suffer. He saw at once that the room was not wholly in darkness. A candle sputtered on a keg, and the scene its dim light revealed to Bunco Kelly was one he never forgot.
>
> "My hair," he related to Spider Johnson, "was pretty thin. But the few strands I had left stood up and pushed my cap into the air."
>
> On the floor near the ladder lay a man. He was alive but not in the best of health. He was gasping, and every little while made as if to clutch his throat. "What's the matter?" Bunco asked him. The man seemed to hear. He lifted his head a bit, tried to say something, but couldn't.
>
> Bunco now let his lantern play around the room. Propped up against one of many barrels were three men—doubtless corpses, Bunco surmised. Their mouths were open, and so were their eyes, but they were not seeing anything. Lying or dropping in odd postures all over the place were other men. Kelly counted 24 all told. Going from one to another, placing his hand on their brows and listening, he came to the conclusion, hurriedly, that at least a third of them still lived. Still, he could not be sure, for he thought that as he watched one of the men gave a deep heave and died.

Bunco soon figured out that the men had broken into what they thought was the basement of the saloon, but they'd instead found themselves below the Johnson & Sons Undertaking Parlors next door. The potent beverage they'd been sipping on, from the kegs there, was not rotgut whiskey but straight formaldehyde.

Feeling dizzy, Bunco ran to the exit to clear his head. "By God," he reportedly exclaimed to himself, "them stiffs has been drinking undertakers' dope!"

It does not seem to have occurred to Bunco that some of the still living victims might yet survive if given prompt medical attention. Perhaps they were truly too far gone; formaldehyde is, of course, lethal stuff. But no, Bunco's first thought seems to have been for the business opportunities the situation presented.

First, he closed the door, so that nobody else would be likely to stumble upon the party; after all, it would not do to have such valuable commodities rescued by some wandering nocturnal do-gooder. Then he set about putting together the logistical support he would need to get two dozen dead and almost-dead guys down to the waterfront and on board ship. He rousted four or five friends, got them down to a livery stable and hired a bunch of cabs.

Back the crew raced to the scene, and they set up a human chain to bring the dead and the dying up the ladder and into the waiting hacks. There was much grumbling among the ranks until Bunco promised five dollars to each of his helpers "after these sailors are aboard ship." After that, things went fast, and soon the cabs were racing across the cobblestones of Portland, headed for the waterfront, to a British barque that Holbrook identifies as the *Flying Prince*—I have found no record of any ship by that name, but it may have been a nickname for a ship with a name like *Prince Edward* or *Crown Prince*.

So, the story goes, Bunco and his pals lugged all two dozen of these bodies onto the ship, convinced the captain that he'd accidentally ordered twenty-four instead of twenty-two, collected thirty dollars per head in blood money and went on their way.

It's about an eight-hour journey down the Columbia to the sea today, chugging along in a modern freighter. In 1893, under sail or being pulled by a steam tug, it took a little longer than that. By the time the ship had reached Astoria, the grisly discovery had been made, and it set off a huge uproar—so the story goes.

The fact is, though, that I haven't been able to find any evidence of such an uproar. In fact, I haven't been able to find any contemporary evidence that anything like this happened at all. Other local historians, so far as I know, haven't either. If this story is true, it most definitely did not happen in 1893. There's no reference to this incident in the Astoria or Portland papers from 1893, and there is not even a passing mention of it in the coverage of Bunco's murder trial in late 1894. The date of this episode has also varied from account to account, ranging from 1885 to 1894, so it is possible that the story, or something like it, happened in the mid- to late 1880s.

Most likely, the story has at least some basis in fact. The story had widespread currency in Portland in the 1930s, when many people still remembered the 1880s well; if it had been wholly made up, someone would have squawked, and so far as I've been able to learn, no one ever did.

It's a fantastic bit of folklore. But what really happened clearly differs from the legend, probably by quite a bit.

SHANGHAI LAW

One thing that we can be sure of is that something like this could have happened in 1890s Portland. You would think that lugging bodies wrapped in tarps to the waterfront and loading them aboard ships would have generated a little official attention, but it wouldn't—not in 1890s Portland. The crimps—and the other shady dealers of the North End—had some friendly faces on the three-man Portland Police Commission, including that of Jonathan Bourne Jr.

The full story of the police commission is in the sixth chapter, but the important thing to know here is that the Portland city government actually had no control over its police department—that was vested in the police commission, which answered to the state governor, who had bigger fish to fry anyway and meddled very little.

So, no, hauling unconscious sailors around the waterfront wouldn't have even raised eyebrows in 1893. In fact, Holbrook reported that one of Portland's police chiefs (this would have to have been Chief Samuel Parrish) actually lost his job in the early '90s after an occupant got shanghaied out of the city jail; the jailbird turned out to be from an influential family. It's hard to know for sure if this is true, since the dismissal/resignation would have been handled on the pretext of something less embarrassing and illegal. But it's probably safe to assume that at least a few obscure drunks were cashed in—if not by the chief himself then certainly by one or two line cops.

Jonathan Bourne Jr., of course, had deep connections in the North End, as well as in the other parts of downtown Portland where graft, corruption, sin and voter fraud could be found. One of his most productive of such contacts was our old invisible friend Larry Sullivan.

Jonathan and Larry had a beautiful friendship. Larry supplied a small army of sailors, who would march around town stuffing a ballot in every ballot box marked in whatever way Jonathan might wish; in return, Jonathan gave Larry political and law enforcement cover, as well as a princely sum on a per-vote basis—rumored to be $2.50, which was enough to purchase fifty schooners of beer at Erickson's Saloon, the legendary loggers' joint at Second and Burnside.

Larry kept a fairly low profile, unlike Bunco. If Bunco was the Bugsy Siegel of Portland crimps, Larry was the Meyer Lansky. The political astuteness he showed was something Bunco never developed.

Larry was quick to discover that running a boardinghouse full of transient people with no permanent address and no real form of identification made him an important political asset, and that became the basis of his relationship with Bourne. His sailors could vote many times in multiple places around town and would do so for the price of a pint if asked; the underworld they were part of mixed so little with mainstream society that it didn't much matter how big their mouths were. His connections on the waterfront made it possible for him to assemble blocs of voters from outside his boardinghouse as well—loggers and hobos and traveling salesmen. Once he enfranchised the entire crew of a Dutch sailing ship that happened to be in port. None of the sailors could speak English, but they all voted a straight "Jonathan Bourne and Friends" ticket when instructed to do so.

But Larry quickly recognized the threat posed to his plans by the flashiness of his then-friend Bunco. Bunco's reputation, and especially his continuing association with the incompetent but brazen Blum-Dunbar opium smuggling operation in early '93 (see the eighth chapter), drew a lot of attention to the boardinghouse operators and their allies in the police department— attention that had the potential to cost a lot of people a lot of money.

Politics intervened as well. As Larry became a key operative of Republican Bourne in the North End, his relations with Bunco, an active Democrat, started getting rockier. And although Bunco and Larry had been great pals at the end of '92—Bunco had bailed Larry out of the hoosegow after he was arrested for punching the harbor master, a man named Byrne, on December 9 of that year—the two of them would be bitter enemies just one year later, and Bunco would end up getting the worst of it by far.

THE SHANGHAIERS' GUILD

Sullivan was apparently something of an organizational genius. Once Bunco Kelly was safely off in the state pen, Sullivan methodically engineered a system in which he and his fellow crimps acquired a stunning amount of control over shipboard labor. The protection afforded by his connection to Bourne made it possible. Essentially, he formed the Portland boardinghouse operators into something like a demonic version of a labor union.

Just before the turn of the century, word started coming back to home ports around the world of a reign of terror on the Portland waterfront—which had always been pretty bad, but not like this.

"You cannot believe how these fellows are working," the captain of the German steel barque *Alsterufer* wrote in a letter home to Hamburg, according to Richard H. Dillon in *Shanghaiing Days*. "It almost seems as though they hold the whole law and authorities in their hands. Sullivan himself said to the German consul, 'I am the law in Portland!'"

The real objections of these captains, and the subsequent diplomatic protests lodged by their national governments, had little if anything to do with any real humanitarian concerns for their crews. Quite the contrary—the protests came after the crimps did something that actually helped the sailors out a little.

Up through the early 1890s, crimping worked out to be a pretty good deal for the skippers, especially the British ones. That was because if a crew member deserted, the skipper got to keep any pay that was owing. For the British captains, who paid off their men only in British ports, this represented a big incentive to encourage desertion. So when the skippers brought their ships into the harbor, they were happy to see the launches and rowboats carrying the boardinghouse runners out to meet them. They might make some token objection, but as the runners passed out bottles and urged the men to climb over the side into the smaller boat, they'd turn their heads and smile.

That all ended in the late 1890s, when the crimps figured out how to force the captains to hand over that money. Basically, they were getting the sailors paid the wages that were due them, which the captains had previously been able to pocket when a man deserted in port. Naturally, this chilled the formerly cozy relationship between the crimps and the captains.

Here's how it worked: The crimps would coach the sailors to commit some minor offense—breaking a window, maybe, or perhaps petty theft. Friends in the district attorney's office would ensure that the sailors drew a little jail time.

A busy day in Portland's harbor. Judging by the ratio of sailing ships to steam vessels, this image was likely made in the late 1890s or early 1900s—the heyday of Larry Sullivan's influence in Portland. *OSU Archives.*

The important thing was for the sailor to be in jail when his ship was ready to leave, because that would constitute a legitimate excuse not to have to report for duty. Thus, when the time came for the ship to leave, its skipper would have to either wait for him to be released or leave the sailor's pay for him, because he was perfectly willing to report for duty but was being legally prevented from doing so—and therefore he was not considered a deserter. The crimp would then hand the wages over to the sailor who'd earned them—taking a hefty cut for his trouble, of course.

If, on the other hand, the sailor had stayed out of jail and simply chose not to show up—which is how it had always worked before—that would constitute desertion, and all wages still owed the sailor would be forfeited.

The crimp would then arrange for the sailor to be released from jail the day after the ship sailed. It was a classic win-win—the sailor got a little extra money to blow and a little more time in town to blow it, and the crimp got a whole new revenue stream. The big losers, of course, were the captains, who suddenly found their entire shore-side crews incarcerated on ridiculous charges like stealing a spittoon or soliciting prostitution, just in time for sailing day.

By about 1901, the crimps' relationship with captains was frankly and openly adversarial, and the captains had to either play ball with the crimps or suffer long and costly delays and difficulty in getting a crew. Ships' officers didn't like this, but most of them didn't resist. Under Sullivan, the crimps could make things very unpleasant for them.

"As soon as they get a seaman ashore they fill him with whisky or some sort of poison which takes a man's senses away," wrote Thomas Manson, owner and captain of the British ship *Penthesilea*, according to author Dillon, "and then they get him into their house and ask him all sorts of questions about the ship, captain and officers, and try if they cannot get a case up to *claim the wages from the ship*. The only way to keep sailors here is to have the boarding masters shot or to drive them out of the place, as they are men of no principle whatever." (Emphasis mine. The wages Captain Manson is referring to are the ones belonging to his sailors, which he had hoped to keep after writing them off as deserters or at least not have to pay until he got back to Liverpool. Seen in that light, his last remark seems a little ironic.)

"There is a gang of boarding masters here who appear to do as they please and run the town to suit their purposes," reported J.A. Patterson, captain of the 329-foot, 3,300-ton four-masted barque *Dunstaffnage*. "They have been able to put into place a mayor, a harbor master and a chief of police who uphold or wink at their nefarious practices."

"The reason I could not write you a sailing letter from Portland was because I had to go into hiding until the ship got to sea," wrote Captain S.P. Hearn of the 1,852-ton British barque *Genista* in 1901, after finding himself the target of Sullivan's crimps and their local law enforcement allies.

On this occasion, though, Hearn got the last laugh—something that didn't happen very often.

COMEUPPANCES FOR THE CRIMPS

The story started when the crimps, apropos of nothing, had Captain Hearn arrested on a charge of criminal libel. Hearn was puzzled by the whole affair until Sullivan and fellow boardinghouse operator Peter Grant came to see him in jail. Please, the crimps said, don't take this personally. They had nothing against the skipper himself, they assured him. Their goal was simply to get back at the ship's owners—Sandback, Tinne & Company of Liverpool—for some past offense.

Once the matter got in front of a grand jury, it was dismissed, and Sullivan and Grant diligently trumped up another legal hassle for Hearn, getting a warrant issued for his arrest to face a civil trial for $10,000 worth of "damage to their reputation." But Hearn, who must have been expecting something like this, had gone into hiding immediately upon his release, and when the sheriff came to fetch him back again, he was nowhere to be found. The crimps prowled around looking for him, offering a $100 reward for his arrest.

Hearn and the crimps played cat-and-mouse for a few days. Then the intrepid captain found a telephone and launched a delightfully enterprising escape plan. First, he called a tugboat operator and asked to have his ship towed out to an anchorage near the Washington side of the Columbia River. Then he sent a friend to charter for him a fast steam launch, to rendezvous with him about five miles east of town after dark. Another friend loaded him in a buggy and raced through the streets with him hidden inside, arriving a little after dark in a thick fog.

After an eventful night featuring a hide-and-seek game on the river with the Multnomah County sheriff—who had heard about the plan—Hearn managed to stow away on the tugboat (with its skipper's permission, of course) as it towed the *Genista* down the river toward the sea. In the middle of the river, Hearn clambered up a boarding ladder and took his command gratefully across the bar and out to sea. One imagines him on the deck, shaking imaginary dust from his feet as the headland at Cape Disappointment fades into the distance behind.

There were a few other times things didn't go the crimps' way, too. In his book, Dillon tells a story of a young man named George Banks who made an arrangement with a ship on the Columbia to deliver some boxes upstream to a railroad project he was working on. Once on board, he was advised that he should consider himself a sailor now and that they'd be going downstream, not up.

"You ain't goin' to shanghai me," Banks retorted, reaching into his pocket. "I'll blow you to hell first."

The hand came out of the pocket full of blasting caps. The boxes? Dynamite. Checkmate: the ship's skipper turned around and headed upstream to Banks's destination, where he unloaded his dynamite, paid for his passage as agreed and was on his way.

Few other shanghai victims or deep-water skippers had such good fortune, though. Actually, most ship captains were under standing orders to do whatever they had to do to get out of Portland on time and with a full crew, even if that full crew should consist of a higher percentage of hayseed farmers and pitch-stained loggers than it had before arrival.

THE END OF THE SHANGHAI ERA

Crimping came to an end in Portland in the first decade or two of the twentieth century, the victim of two great trends: first, the triumph of steam power over sail, and second, the triumph of a former seaman turned union organizer named Andrew Furuseth, president of the International Seamen's Union.

Furuseth dedicated his life to the cause of emancipating sailors from their indentured servitude. He finally accomplished this in 1915 when Congress passed the Seaman's Act, the "Magna Carta of the sea," which revolutionized the life of a sailor. Control that sailors gained over their own lives was control the crimps lost. At the same time, the old labor-intensive windjammers were

A steamship gets loaded with wheat at a Portland wharf, using conveyer belts, circa 1910. The switch from sails to steam eventually drove the shanghai operators out of business, postcard image.

disappearing from the harbor, and the steamers that replaced them were far safer and more comfortable to work aboard. For the first time in fifty years, a life as a merchant mariner was becoming a career a man might choose rather than a fate that might overtake him if he was not careful.

Steamship skippers found they could simply hire crews directly, without dealing with the boarding masters at all. And, of course, the more men started hiring directly on to ships, the less need there was to resort to kidnapping and extortion to fill out crews.

And so the golden age of crimping in Portland slowly faded away. Spider Johnson told Holbrook that there were three gangs of crimps still struggling to survive in Portland on the eve of the First World War, supplying the few tattered tall ships still in operation. Captain P.A. McDonald of the barque *Moshulu* told Dillon that he'd had to work with a crimp who called himself Shanghai White to get a crew for a voyage from Portland to Australia as late as 1928. But by about 1930, crimping was history.

ofor.us/wp06

Fixing the Police

In Portland's first fifty years of existence, the quality of law enforcement improved dramatically—from "extremely sketchy" to "just sketchy." This was probably to be expected; the city was simply growing too fast, and a police presence that was okay one year would be woefully inadequate a few years on. It was constantly playing catch-up.

The need for a police force became painfully obvious almost immediately upon the city's founding. Historian Jewel Lansing quotes an April 1851 article in the *Weekly Oregonian*: "On Thursday a serious and brutal riot again disgraced our city. Several of the hands from the steamer Goliath became intoxicated and commenced a general fight on shore among themselves which resulted in the biting-off of a piece of the nose of George Robbin, coal heaver, who in return stabbed with a dirk knife Henry Wood, fireman, in several places."

There were also several violent private feuds being carried out at that time. Clearly something needed to be done. So at the city council meeting that month, the council members voted to hire a military man named Hiram Wilber—who, a few years later, would lead Company B of the Oregon Rangers—as Portland's first city marshal.

Wilber quit two months later and was replaced by a twenty-eight-year-old sailor named William L. Higgins. The record is scant on the accomplishments of this city marshal, but one gleans from subtle hints here and there that there was a certain dissatisfaction with Higgins's performance.

"We are creditably informed that our city is at this time infested with several professed blacklegs [crooked gamblers], who are in the habit of inveigling

A political cartoon critical of Portland's police, published in 1889. *From* The West Shore *magazine.*

into their den and swindling persons who can be induced to risk money upon the turn of a card," the *Portland Oregonian* noted gloomily in November 1852. "We now have an efficient mayor and a full board of aldermen, and ought to have a city marshal who would ferret out those sporting gentlemen. A few days in the block house on bread and water would have a tendency to purge our city from these bejeweled worthless[es]."

The ironic thing is that future city marshal and police chief James Lappeus was probably one of the "blacklegs" the *Oregonian* was complaining about so bitterly.

The following year, the paper went so far as to suggest that perhaps, if the marshal could not or would not do something about the "disgraceful midnight rows and bacchanalian revelry, by a group of vagabonds hanging around the low groggeries in the daytime and destroying property at night," a few armed vigilante committees would take care of the problem for them. Fortunately, this suggestion doesn't seem to have been acted upon.

For the rest of the decade, Portland went through marshals at an average rate of one every eleven months. Higgins, the ex-sailor, came back briefly in '54 and again in '56. James Lappeus was there in '59 and stayed until '61,

Downtown Portland just a few years after its founding, in 1851. This was seven years before the Danford Balch murder. *OSU Archives.*

long enough to preside over the notorious Danford Balch murder, and came back again for a year in '68. The longest-serving marshal was Henry Hoyt.

The era of city marshals in Portland ended in 1870, when the police department was created.

THE DANFORD BALCH CASE

The Danford Balch case was Portland's first high-profile murder case and its first official execution—and it cast a long, sinister shadow over the rest of James Lappeus's law enforcement career.

Danford Balch was a crusty homesteader who had perfected a claim on a piece of very hilly real estate just northwest of Portland—actually, the old Balch property included some of the most valuable real estate in present-day Portland. Balch had a daughter, fifteen-year-old Anna Balch, who had fallen for a young fellow named Mortimer Stump while Mortimer was working on the Balch place. Balch, realizing what was going on and apparently taking a dim view of Mortimer as a prospective son-in-law, kicked the young Lothario off the property, but shortly thereafter, Anna ran away with Mortimer and the two of them got married. This was in November 1858.

After the elopement, Anna and Mortimer laid low for a week or so, living with Stump's parents on their farm northeast of Portland, but eventually they had to come to town to buy supplies. Perhaps fearing for their safety if they didn't appear in force, the entire Stump family came to town. When they did, they had the bad luck to encounter Balch in onetime Portland mayor Addison Starr's general store.

The week and a half that had elapsed since Anna ran away had done Balch no good at all. He had, according to his writings, barely slept at all and had spent the entire time brooding and fuming. This pent-up fury now vented itself in a heated exchange with Mortimer Stump's father, who responded to the torrent of abuse by shouting back that Anna Balch was just "a common little bitch." This remark—quoted verbatim in Danford Balch's jailhouse diary later on—seems to have set the old man off. He raced home and retrieved his double-barreled shotgun. Before heading back to town with it, he also threw back a couple stiff drinks. Actually, he may have thrown back more than just a couple.

Balch caught up with the Stump family as they were boarding the Stark Street Ferry for the crossing into what would someday be East Portland, for the journey home. There, in broad daylight in front of dozens of witnesses, he emptied the contents of both shotgun barrels into young Mortimer. An instant later, poor Anna was both a widow and an orphan-to-be.

Arrested and taken to the primitive and rickety building that then served as Portland's municipal lockup, Danford Balch spent a few months in jail and then escaped and spent a few more months hiding out in what today is Forest Park, with his family and friends feeding him; in the meantime, Lappeus was elected marshal.

In July, Lappeus learned where Balch was hiding and went and arrested him. Balch was brought to trial almost immediately. In court, Balch claimed that he had intended only to kidnap Anna, not to shoot anyone, and that the gun had gone off accidentally (twice).

As a defense against a murder rap, this story worked about as well as you'd think it would, and the following month, Balch went through the floor of the gallows in Portland's first-ever public hanging. To the shocked disapproval of the *Morning Oregonian*, the hanging was attended by a dry-eyed Anna (Balch) Stump.

And that was the end of that…or so most people thought. Two years later, when Lappeus was up for reelection, a man named Richard Loney stepped forward and publicly accused Lappeus of having offered to free Balch from the city jail for a $1,000 bribe. This, Loney said, came after Balch had been convicted and while he was awaiting execution. Loney backed up his claim with several affidavits from people swearing that Balch's wife tried desperately but unsuccessfully to raise the cash.

Was this true? Well, Lappeus was, as we know, no angel. Certainly it would have been no particularly difficult thing for the city marshal to "accidentally" leave the jail unlocked for the night, and the West Coast was a big place in 1858, easy for a wanted man to get lost in. There's no compelling reason to doubt the accusations, although they probably wouldn't have held up in court.

True or not, the claim clung to Lappeus for the rest of his career in law enforcement like a dormant malaria parasite, finally flaring up twenty-four years later at the behest of corrupt Mayor Chapman in a successful bid to replace him as chief of police.

The Portland Police Department

In 1870, the city council decided that Portland needed a real police department and asked City Marshal Joseph Saunders to help draw up the necessary rules and structures. However, at the same time, the Oregon state legislature in Salem was in the process of seizing control of the whole thing. Fearful that stagecoach/railroad mogul Ben Holladay was about to take over the state's largest city, the legislators rammed through a bill creating a three-member police commission whose members they could control. The Portland City Council was literally stripped of all control of its own police department—although it was still required to pay the bills, of course. The new commission then named James Lappeus as Portland's first police chief.

There is some question over whether Lappeus really was Portland's first chief or whether Saunders got to occupy the post for the few weeks (or hours, or minutes…anything would do) before Lappeus's appointment became official. The modern Portland Police Department, not surprisingly, prefers the Saunders version. Saunders was the architect of the department. He was also, by all accounts, a straight and honest cop of the sort a department can be proud to call a founding father, and he sure deserved better than to get kicked aside and have the credit for his labors

Prisoners line up for coffee and breakfast in the Portland City Jail in 1889. Most of these men were probably picked up for public drunkenness the night before. *From* The West Shore *magazine.*

given to an old card-sharping blackleg and gold-field desperado who ran a saloon/theater that, rumor had it, dabbled in prostitution to boot.

It was a rocky start either way. For the first fourteen years of the new police department's life, it was under the direction of either Lappeus or the equally corrupt Luzerne Besser. Along the way, the city managed to regain control of its police department, but the police commissioners were made elected officials—meaning that the city council still didn't have real control over them.

But 1885 saw the takeover of the police commission by the state once again, and this time the situation was, if anything, worse. The governor promptly appointed the three most vice-friendly politicians in Portland to the police commission: Byron Cardwell, Joseph Simon and Jonathan Bourne Jr. Of these three guys, Cardwell was fairly obscure but was a great team player; Simon was the ringleader; and Bourne we've already met.

As police chief, the commission appointed the son of a highly respected pioneer Methodist minister, Samuel B. Parrish. Parrish didn't make too many waves. Although he was once reprimanded and fined $100 for "arresting" wayward boys and girls in an apparent attempt to scare them straight, once those wayward kids had grown up and gone over to the Dark Side, he could be counted on to not bother them much—so long as they stayed in the North End. And, of course, there was that rumor of shanghaiing.

Trouble came around every time the North End people spilled out of those boundaries—as had happened in the late 1880s with Nancy Boggs's maritime exploits, in 1893 with the Blum-Dunbar drug-smuggling operation and in the late 1890s with Liverpool Liz's bicycle-riding trollops. And in those cases, trouble took the form of public pressure on the police department to do something about it. More people scrutinized what the police were doing, opportunities for extracurricular fundraising got fewer and riskier and a police chief had to walk a very fine line. The "business as usual" crowd in Portland didn't want the boat rocked and could be depended on to not back up a chief or commander who got too zealous. Reform-minded mayors only lasted in office until the people of Portland got over their outrage over whatever had called the city's vice to their attention, and after that there might well be hell to pay for a cop who had shut down the wrong brothel and caused somebody named Ladd or Failing or Weinhard to lose a few thousand dollars in rent.

The best policy was to keep the North End people in line so that they wouldn't call attention to themselves while presenting the "respectable" people of Portland with a department that looked and operated like a professional, public service–oriented constabulary. For the most part, Portland cops were successful at this.

ofor.us/wp07

Mayors Behaving Badly

Throughout the second half of the 1800s, Portland enjoyed a fabulous run of bad behavior at the very top of the municipal pecking order—in the office of the mayor. In fact, by the time the town was ten years old, the mayor's office had already produced the cast of characters for a drama that would have brought rave reviews as a vaudeville comedy routine.

1859: MAYOR V. MAYOR

One of the most hotly contested issues in pre–Civil War Portland was whether or not the public owned the levee along the river. The answer, eventually, was no, but in 1859 the issue was still quite hot, and on one particular winter day, an amazing assortment of mayors, ex-mayors, law enforcement officers and members of the general public got involved with something closely resembling a riot over it.

In January 1859, former mayor George Vaughn was busy building a wharf on the riverbank between Alder and Morrison, claiming that he owned the property there. The city, which didn't agree, got a court to order him to stop construction while the ownership issues were worked out. Well, instead of doing that, the ex-mayor finished his project, and by early spring the next year, he'd started construction on a building to enclose the wharf.

The city council issued an order to Vaughn: remove the wharf within twenty-four hours or the town marshal (James Lappeus) would be asked

to remove it. And Lappeus was given a copy of the notice and ordered to serve it on Vaughn.

Lappeus headed down to the levee to do so. When he got there, he found that Vaughn had already heard the news and in response had hired a huge crew of construction workers, big enough to finish the entire project before the end of the day. Lappeus handed over the papers to Vaughn and informed the workers that they were trespassing. No one paid him any heed, and Vaughn defiantly stomped the papers into the mud beneath his feet.

By daylight the next day, ex-mayor Vaughn's wharf and building were complete. But current mayor Stephen McCormick and Marshal Lappeus were on their way down to the waterfront to start the removal process. A showdown was brewing.

Then came a surprise twist. Waiting for them at the waterfront was a third onetime mayor of Portland, Addison Starr, who also happened to be the sheriff of Multnomah County. Upon their arrival, ex-mayor Starr arrested Mayor McCormick and Marshal Lappeus, in execution of ex-mayor Vaughn's warrant. The charge: "Intent to destroy private property."

The charges were quickly dismissed, and both mayor and top city cop were free men within an hour or two. But in the meantime, word had spread, and by now the whole town was pretty riled up. When the two officials charged back down to the waterfront to finish what they'd tried to start, they found themselves at the head of an angry mob, which joyfully reduced ex-mayor Vaughn's building and wharf to their constituent hunks of wood in just a few minutes.

A panoramic drawing of Portland as it appeared from the east side of the river in 1858, the year before ex-mayor Vaughn built his controversial wharf. *J. Gaston,* Portland: Its History and Builders *(1911).*

"Some persons object to the manner of removing the building," opined the *Morning Oregonian* the next day. "If Mr. Vaughn had not, in a defiant manner, manifested a determination to erect the building, in an unusual way, and in such hot haste, with full knowledge that the city authorities and a large portion of the people were opposed to it, and if he had not treated their authority with contempt by trampling their protest under his feet, the building would probably have been rolled off [instead] of demolished."

Vaughn, for his part, angrily shook the dust of Portland from his feet and moved to Vancouver for a time.

City Marshal Law

Throughout the first half of 1867, Mayor Thomas Holmes complained quite a bit about the city marshal. At this time, James Lappeus was no longer in the position—he'd stepped down after the rumors of the alleged Balch bribery scheme started circulating. So when Mayor Holmes complained that the city marshal was ripping the taxpayers off, he was complaining about Marshal Henry Hoyt.

At the time, the marshal was not a city employee; rather, he was an elected official (elected either by the voters or by the city council, depending on which city charter was in place at any given time; the city changed charters frequently in these years). The marshal was compensated more or less on a piecework basis, like an independent contractor. This saved lots of money when things were quiet and still, but it cost the city plenty when the joints started jumping, and apparently Hoyt had figured out that his appointment made it possible for him to hit the cash box hard and often. There was always some kind of crime being committed somewhere, especially on the waterfront.

Unfortunately, Mayor Holmes's complaints did not have the effect for which he had hoped. Instead, they inspired a record turnout of eager (not to say greedy) candidates for the job of city marshal, including one A. Rosenheim, who just happened to also be a member of the Portland City Council. This was a problem because under the city charter that was in place at the time, the city council appointed the marshal.

Rosenheim got four colleagues to join him in his vote for himself, and at the August meeting of the city council, he was declared the city marshal. Unfortunately, Marshal Hoyt refused to hand over the office, saying that Rosenheim had been illegally elected.

The council then filed suit against Hoyt, asking a judge to order him out. The case worked its way up to the Oregon Supreme Court, which ruled—quite logically—that it was not okay for a member of an executive board to use his appointing power to place himself in a lucrative job.

Having made his point, Hoyt stepped down from the job a few months later.

CO-MAYORS OF PORTLAND

In 1881, upstart attorney Joseph Simon—a good friend of Jonathan Bourne and, a few years after this, one of Bourne's fellow police commissioners—was running for mayor against incumbent mayor David Thompson. When the polls closed, election judges announced that Simon had won by 9 votes out of 3,570. Naturally, there was a review of the ballots by the city auditor, county clerk and justice of the peace. They determined that Simon had in fact lost by 1 vote: 1,784 to 1,785.

Simon, ignoring this bit of bad news, demanded that the council declare him the winner anyway. The council struggled to figure out what the right thing to do might be, as the mighty *Morning Oregonian* thundered away every day, demanding that it declare Thompson reelected. A recount was clearly in order.

But there was another problem. It seemed that City Councilor William Andrus had a little money riding on the outcome.

Andrus denied it, but five different people filed affidavits swearing that he'd bet on Simon to win. Andrus's response was a couple more affidavits

The view in 1888 looking north on Second Street from Yamhill Street, including the offices of *The West Shore* magazine and Oregon Historical Society founding father George Himes; across the street is the office of the short-lived *Portland Daily News*. *From* The West Shore *magazine.*

from people swearing that yeah, okay, Andrus had bet on Simon, but the wagers were on their behalf and not his own. This sounded just as plausible in 1881 as it sounds today.

Andrus's betting was certainly irregular, but it wasn't a real problem until after the recount results came in. The recount confirmed that Thompson had won by one vote, but it excluded two disputed ballots that were cast for Simon. If those ballots were counted, Simon won by one vote. And, of course, it was safe to assume that Andrus himself had voted for Simon, too. Should his vote be thrown away? What to do?

The council met to discuss both disputed ballots, one by one. On the first, Simon's name had been written over Thompson's. The council awarded the ballot to Simon. The two men were now tied. As for the next ballot, it's not clear what was wrong with it, but after due consideration, the city council voted on it. The result was four votes to give it to Simon and four votes to throw it out.

Finally, after a clumsy and futile attempt to toss this hot potato over to the Supreme Court, the council voted again. This time, council decided to throw it out by a vote of five to three. The two mayoral candidates remained tied with 1,783 votes each. The council then tabled Simon's request to be declared mayor, and Thompson was left in the office by default.

Presumably, Andrus lost his money, but on this point the historical record is, mercifully, silent.

MAYOLA

In 1882, a physician named James Chapman was elected mayor. He'd already served two nonconsecutive terms as mayor; both times, his tenure was more or less unremarkable. But this, his third and final term, would be different.

Things started out innocently enough, although there were some odd things about it. For one thing, remember that allegation that then-marshal James Lappeus had offered to spring convicted murderer Danford Balch for a $1,000 bribe twenty-two years earlier? For some reason, that old allegation was suddenly back in the news.

The city council investigated and cleared Lappeus of the charges, but Mayor Chapman canned him anyway. The council then installed William A. Watkinds as chief.

A few months later, Chapman publicly confessed that he had bought his election. It seemed he had cut a deal with ex-chief of police and former city council member Luzerne Besser, who had given him $1,000 in gold in exchange for a written promise to appoint Besser as superintendent of the streets and one of Besser's cronies, Thomas Connell, as chief of police. Obediently, Chapman had dug up the old Balch incident and used it as a pretext to fire Lappeus. But then the council had nominated Watkinds by a veto-proof majority, and Chapman had been unable to come through on the deal. Besser then started blackmailing him, so Chapman put an end to that by confessing the whole thing.

And resigning in disgrace, right? Right?

Surely by now you know enough about early Portland politics to know better than that. No, Besser firmly announced he planned to stay.

"You know that such bargains are made before every election," he insisted, by way of claiming that what he'd done was no big deal. "Presidents of the United States do it too."

According to this bargain, Besser had promised to nominate Chapman for mayor, furnish him the $1,000 and then, after his election, use his influence with the legislature to get the mayor a $5,000 annual salary. If that lobbying effort failed, Besser would pay Chapman $1,000 per year to, as the contract puts it with a wink and a nudge, "compensate him for his time and trouble and loss of time and certain incidental expenses that will naturally occur in discharging the onerous duties of the office of mayor of this city."

In exchange, Chapman had agreed to set Besser and Connell up with plum city jobs. This he had apparently failed to do for either one of them.

So the city council had a problem. If Chapman refused to leave, the council could hire an attorney and legally force him out…if it could afford it. The members could also vote to fire him, but he had vowed to veto that vote, and he still had enough supporters on the council that it could not override his veto.

So Mayor Chapman served out the remainder of his term and left office quietly, with no charges filed and few questions asked.

"SYLPESTER ANNOYER"

Sylvester Pennoyer was the name of the mayor elected in 1896, and he had a bit of a history. In fact, he was a two-term ex-governor of Oregon.

Pennoyer was originally an attorney who'd come to Portland from back east to teach in one of its earliest schools. He'd gotten in on the ground floor in the lumber processing business and was now worth a big pile. He was also utterly nuts.

A pugnacious racist, Pennoyer had no use for the Chinese and felt that the abolition of slavery had been a terrible mistake. He wore the most formal plutocratic attire possible—black suits with swallow-tail coats, formal top hats, a gold watch and chain—but talked and acted like a rabble-rousing labor-unionist or a proto-Wobbly.

He'd gotten elected governor in 1886 by crashing someone else's political campaign rally, seizing control and turning it into a wild, slogan-chanting, brick-throwing anti-Chinese riot. Then, after leading the mob for several days of fairly scary demonstrations, he'd started urging them to "seek relief at the ballot," which, conveniently enough, he turned out to be on. And so was elected Oregon's most controversial governor ever.

Duties in Salem took Pennoyer away from his city for a few years, during which time his reputation went nationwide. Mostly, he made his name by feuding with sitting presidents. In 1892, he famously sent a telegram to President William McKinley telling him to mind his own business—his exact words were, "I will attend to my business. Let the president attend to his." When the next president, Benjamin Harrison, came to Oregon, Pennoyer kept him waiting in the rain for ten minutes at the Salem railroad depot before arriving to meet him in an outrageously showy carriage drawn by four white horses.

In Salem, former governor T.T. Geer wrote later, Pennoyer said and did things that were "absurd in the extreme and created great merriment in the Legislature and out of it." One such absurdity earned Pennoyer a new nickname—and cemented his reputation for utter nuttiness—when he vetoed a bill that would have enabled Portland to finance its new Bull Run water project with $500,000 worth of bonds. His reasoning: Bull Run water originated in glacier runoff, and consequently it would, he claimed, "cause goiter to the fair sex of Portland." Judge Matthew Deady, who had put in plenty of work on this bill, was so put out that he wrote in his diary that Pennoyer "ought to be called Sylpester Annoyer."

The fact was, by blocking the Bull Run project, Pennoyer was putting "the fair sex of Portland" at a real risk of worse things than goiter—cholera, for instance. Like many towns of the day, Portland got much of its water from the Willamette River. But unlike those other towns, Portland was downstream from every other community in the Willamette Valley, and all of them shot their sewage untreated straight into the waterway. Add to that the thousands of cattle grazing right along the riverbanks, and all the wild animals to boot, and it's easy to see why most Portlanders were really looking forward to getting clean tap water.

The legislature came within one vote of overriding Pennoyer's veto, but that didn't make the bill any less dead—or Deady any less mad.

Several years after that, Pennoyer was elected mayor of Portland, and he was in that job when the new Bull Run water project was completed and ready for use. Luckily for the allegedly goiter-prone "fair sex of Portland," the proponents of the Bull Run project had figured out another way to get the job done.

In an ironic twist, as the city's top executive, it fell to Pennoyer to take the ceremonial first sip from the water supply that he had tried to prevent from being tapped. And he executed this duty with typical Sylvester Pennoyer grace and flair—which is to say, with not much of either but with great and possibly unintentional humor. He took a healthy swig, set the goblet down and grumbled, "No flavor. No body. Give me the old Willamette."

ofor.us/wp08

World's Dumbest
Drug Smugglers

I n 2002, a man named Gabriel Scott suddenly realized that the strangely shaped formation he was looking at, sticking up out of the mud of Alaska's Inside Passage about fifty miles south of Cordoba, was the steam engine of a sunken ship.

The ship turned out to be an old one: a small, wooden-hulled steamship with a screw propeller, dating back to the late 1800s. It had been buried in silt and sand until an earthquake in 1964 heaved the ground upward a good twelve feet. Since that time, erosion had been peeling away the dirt covering the old ship, and now it was finally exposed.

Two years later, the TV show *History Detectives* sent a crew out to investigate. They thought that it might possibly be the SS *Portland*, the ship that launched the Yukon Gold Rush when it showed up in Seattle in 1897 with the famous "ton of gold" on board.

They were right.

There was much rejoicing in Alaska; for that state, the *Portland* was a sort of historian's Holy Grail. For several years after that historic 1897 run, the *Portland* was the most important steamer on the West Coast, shuttling thousands of hopeful miners from Seattle to Alaska en route to the Klondike and, later, Nome.

For Alaska, there is no other ship with as much historical and cultural significance. But it's also a pretty significant part of the history of the city it was named after. You see, before the steamer was purchased by a Seattle company and renamed the *Portland*, it was known as the SS *Haytian Republic*, and it was the most notorious smuggling ship on the West Coast. It was operated by a gang of smugglers whose clumsiness and ineptitude were like something out of a Buster Keaton–era silent comedy, so its name was in the newspapers a lot. Every reader in Portland knew that steamer.

THE SHIP

The *Haytian Republic* was built in Bath, Maine, in 1885. It was a small, svelte steamer, 191 feet long and less than one thousand tons; nominally, it was built for the West Indies trade, but in reality it was probably built specifically as a blockade runner. At the time, the island nation of Haiti was in near-constant civil war; there was good money to be made running guns and food past the Haitian government's blockade and trading them with rebel groups for coffee, sugar and other Caribbean goodies, and there was a cadre of maritime Yankee traders that was happy to make that money, even if it was a bit dangerous. These traders had a number of small, fast steamers built with an eye to outrunning the Haitian government gunboats and—on those occasions when it felt like intervening—the U.S. Navy.

After working this dangerous trade for a few years, the *Haytian Republic* was seized by the U.S. government and brought around the horn, where it was acquired by a Portland outfit called the Merchants Steamship Company.

THE SMUGGLERS

In 1892, the Merchants Steamship Company was owned primarily by two men: William Dunbar and Nat Blum. The two of them also had a wholesale grocery outfit called Dunbar Produce and Grocery, located just south of Burnside on Front Street in the North End. Dunbar, the senior partner, was actually a former business associate of Jonathan Bourne Jr.'s, having been the secretary on the board of directors of a textile company that Bourne founded in the late 1880s.

Merchants Steamship owned two ships: the *Haytian Republic* and the *Wilmington*, both of them small, fast ex–blockade runners. It kept these two ships very busy, shuttling back and forth to Victoria, British Columbia, bringing in groceries for Dunbar Produce, as well as lots of "passengers"—Chinese passengers.

Dunbar and Blum ran their steamships for about two years, smuggling both illegal Chinese immigrants and black-market opium. Their exploits culminated in a sensational trial during which fifteen people—eight of them federal customs and port officials and one of them the leader of the Oregon Republican Party—were tried on federal charges.

The West Shore's staff artist's 1889 drawing of Chinese laborers being smuggled into Oregon in the middle of the night. Dunbar and Blum, of course, preferred a less discreet, more flamboyant approach to smuggling. *From* The West Shore *magazine.*

During that trial, Blum turned state's evidence and started naming names and telling stories. In the process, he gave the city of Portland a December to remember in 1893, dropping a fresh bombshell for the newspapers to titter about nearly every day that month.

The biggest bit of news was the involvement of the head of the Oregon Republican Party, Stark Street Ferry co-owner James Lotan. Lotan, who had until the scandal broke out enjoyed a cushy federal appointment as customs collector for the Port of Portland, stood accused of using his good offices badly by helping Blum and Dunbar smuggle thousands of Chinese workers and tons of Chinese opium into Oregon in return for a healthy cut of the action.

Portland was riveted. The rest of the country was pretty interested, too.

In court, Blum told the judge that he had known Lotan for several years, and one day Lotan approached him with what you might call an open-ended business opportunity. Lotan, it seemed, had learned that he was about to receive his appointment as customs collector. That meant he would be the top official in charge of making sure that no smuggling was done. Naturally, this presented tremendous opportunities for a fellow who didn't mind engaging in a bit of smuggling himself. Kind of like an exclusive franchise.

"Lotan asked how it could be done and I told him that there were a number of Chinese laborers who wanted to come into the United States that could afford to pay him $50 a head," Blum told the court, according to the *Portland Evening Telegram*'s account of the proceedings. ($50 in 1893 would be equivalent to about $1,275 today.)

A mutually profitable understanding was soon reached, Blum testified, and when Lotan was confirmed as customs collector, the smugglers threw a big party for him, with Chinese fireworks and lots of food and drink. (Lotan, of course, denied all this.)

Soon, Blum claimed, they had a running operation. With the help of Lotan's department, they generated a stack of forged paperwork to be handed out to the paying customers. Each Chinese laborer would pony up $120 and would be taken to one of the Canadian cities of Vancouver or Victoria. There they would finalize the forged papers with pictures and anything else needed before heading south toward Portland.

"On the way over here, [Chinese smugglers posing as cooks on the *Haytian Republic* or *Wilmington*] instructed the Chinamen on every point they were to be cross-examined upon by the collector," Blum said. "They were told of the witnesses to their identity, what firm they belonged to, the amount of money they had as a share where they did business, how long they had been away

The Wild and Lusty Underworld of a Frontier Seaport Town

The Portland waterfront shortly after the turn of the century, with four bridges proudly on display, postcard image.

from the United States, which direction the streets run and everything they would be asked upon their arrival here."

It was, truth be told, a slick operation, and if Blum and Dunbar had confined themselves to smuggling just illegal immigrants, they might have turned out okay. But of course, they did not.

There was more money in smuggling opium than immigrants. At the time, opium was not actually illegal, but it was subject to a punishing import duty of twelve dollars per pound; sneaking black-market dope into the country was a big business, and the Chinese communities in Portland and San Francisco at the time consumed large amounts of it. The steamers were making the trip anyway, and an extra half ton of cargo wouldn't make a difference. It must have seemed like a natural fit.

Their scheme was this: the *Wilmington* or *Haytian Republic* would put into port in Portland. By now they were well known there as suspicious operators, so they would be examined closely; Lotan might be a friend, but he could not be seen to be favoring people whom everyone knew were smugglers. But that would be okay because by the time they got inspected, the dope would be long gone—chucked overboard in barrels a few miles downriver, for other members of the gang to retrieve.

Now, this might sound like a fairly workable plan. But as the old computer hackers' saying goes, nothing is foolproof to a sufficiently talented fool. It turned out there were a number of ways in which things might go wrong.

SPECIAL MISDELIVERY

They went wrong on July 28, 1892, when gang member Robert Garthorn bought three hundred pounds of opium in Victoria, loaded it on the *Wilmington* and returned to Portland by rail. As planned, he arrived before the steamer's scheduled arrival time, and he and another smuggler, H. Thomas Berg, went down to meet the steamer off St. Johns, where it was scheduled to lay its big wooden barrel–shaped eggs.

The steamer was scheduled to arrive sometime between midnight and dawn, but it didn't. Finally, no doubt exhausted, Garthorn and Berg gave up and went back to Portland. A few hours later, the steamer came along, and its chief engineer rolled the three big barrels off into the drink, just as planned. But nobody was there to receive them.

When Blum and Dunbar heard about this, they sprang into panicky action. Blum and another gang member ran to rent a steam launch and headed downriver with it, picking up Garthorn on the way. Soon they saw one of their precious barrels sitting on an old dock, and they pulled in and

Front Street at its intersection with C Street—now known as Couch Street—looking southward. Dunbar Produce and Grocery would have been about three blocks down on the left. *From* The West Shore *magazine*.

introduced themselves to the man who was standing nearby, a river pilot named J.L. Caples.

Mr. Caples had some idea of what they were up to. Although he didn't know what opium looked like, he'd opened the barrel, and what was inside sure looked like it could be opium. (Most likely it was packed in one-tael cans with Chinese characters printed on them. One tael was equal to roughly one and one-third ounces.)

Caples had been watching them making their way down the river, hugging the shore and peering into every inlet, and was pretty sure they were smugglers.

Garthorn, wearing a brass star to look like he might be a customs official, cheerfully offered to pay Caples $1 for his trouble in retrieving the barrel. But Caples, perhaps playing a hunch, counteroffered at $50. Blum only had $10 on him, along with two or three $100 bills—which Caples thought were probably counterfeit. So Blum told Caples to stop by Dunbar Produce and Grocery at 52 Front Street later that day, and there would be $40 waiting for him there.

If Caples had any doubt about who the opium smugglers were in Portland and what business they operated out of, that would have laid it to rest, right there.

THE WILMINGTON GETS BUSTED

Some time later, the steamer *Wilmington* was on its way to Astoria with some opium aboard when Dunbar learned that federal officials knew about it. Hastily, he sent Garthorn out with Bunco Kelly to intercept the ship, but as it crossed the bar, a revenue cutter fell in behind it as a kind of escort. Helplessly, the two men watched from the launch as the steamer tied up in Astoria only to have its 450-pound load of opium seized. The *Wilmington* itself was seized at the same time. The gang would now have to get by on just one steamship—the *Haytian Republic*.

REVENGE OF THE NOSY NEIGHBOR

A month and a half later, on September 2, the smugglers brought in a big shipment on the *Haytian Republic*—1,400 pounds of opium, which was dumped overboard in the Columbia and retrieved by Dunbar himself.

Garthorn and Berg took charge of it and hauled it off to Berg's house, where they busied themselves stashing it inside.

But a day or two before, Berg's wife had gotten into a quarrel with one of the neighbors, and the neighbor apparently had been waiting for this moment. As soon as she saw this big flurry of late-night loading activity, she picked up the telephone (very few people had them in 1893, but she did) to get her revenge by calling the police.

This was lousy timing, since there was more than half a ton of opium in the house at the time. But the call seems to have been fielded by a friend of Nat Blum's, because the police never did show up. Instead, Nat himself did, knocking on the neighbor's door and introducing himself as a police detective.

While "Detective Blum" was taking her statement, the two of them watched Garthorn and Berg through a window as they hauled the opium out of Berg's house and wheeled it down the street on a cart—apparently getting away. But Blum smoothly told the neighbor lady not to worry—the two smugglers were walking right into a trap, he assured her. He told the woman, as the *Telegram* reported, "that he had two policemen stationed down the road, who would catch them with the opium and place them under arrest, thus securing her silence until after the opium had been removed to his own house."

Blum must have been too busy congratulating himself on this smooth play to realize that it meant Berg's house was no longer a safe place to stash contraband. This would prove to be an expensive oversight.

When another big load came in two months later, another half ton went into Berg's house, and Dunbar sent over another four hundred pounds. This they started packing into steamer trunks, one hundred pounds to a trunk, and Blum, along with two other members of the gang, headed to San Francisco, each with two trunks. One of the three got busted there, and the opium was confiscated.

When they got back to Portland, they found that eight hundred pounds of opium had been stolen from Berg's house while they were all gone. It's tempting to wonder if that suspicious neighbor lady, who obviously kept a close eye on the Berg house, had anything to do with it.

A few months later, Dunbar made a trip to San Francisco with two trunks and lost one of the claim checks on the way. Blum found the claim check but was afraid to claim the trunk himself, so he paid another man $300 ($7,600 in 2012 dollars) to go get it. The newspapers don't say whether he was successful or not, so presumably he was.

Another attempt to get the dope to San Francisco was an even bigger fiasco. Dunbar packed several hundred pounds in boxes marked "Playing Cards" and shipped them southward. But the two burly draymen he hired to load the boxes thought it was really weird to be shipping thousands and thousands of boxes of playing cards to a city that was perfectly capable of supplying itself with gambling accouterments, and the next day they told Police Chief Spencer about it. Spencer telegraphed San Francisco, the shipment was stopped and inspected and the Dunbar-Blum gang was busted again. This time, there was a bill of lading with Dunbar Produce and Grocery's name and address on it.

All told, the gang lost at least half a ton of opium in seizures. It lost about twice that much to theft. That's at least 20 percent of all the opium that passed through their hands. They also managed to lose a $30,000 steamer. It's hard to imagine how it all could possibly have penciled out.

BUSTED

As you will have gathered, it didn't exactly take brilliant detective work to figure out what was going on over at Dunbar Produce and Grocery.

It may have been Caples who blew the whistle on the gang. Or perhaps the nosy neighbor with whom Mrs. Berg was feuding sent a letter off to someone in Washington, D.C. Certainly having the Portland chief of police made aware that tons of opium are being shipped out from one's grocery business, packed in playing-card boxes, is never an astute career move for a smuggler. Or maybe it was the man Dunbar hired for three days to search for nine hundred pounds of opium stolen from under a bridge in Albina—that man took a job as a policeman a few months later.

It seems most likely that all of these sources played some role in the getting-out of the proverbial bagged cat. In any case, federal officials soon started getting wise to the gang.

Somewhere along the line, Lotan lost his job as collector of customs. That wasn't necessarily because he was suspected of having had something to do with the smuggling, at least at first; chances are good he was simply fired for incompetence. After all, the most obvious and blatant smuggling operation imaginable had been operating out of his port for months, and he had done nothing to stop it.

But in late November 1893, a grand jury returned indictments against fifteen people—including Lotan himself. The charges involved smuggling

A drawing of the first Steel Bridge, sketched the year before the bridge was opened to the public, linking Portland with Albina, in 1888. Locomotives crossed on the lower deck and pedestrians and buggies above. This bridge was replaced in 1912 with today's Steel Bridge. This might have been the bridge under which smuggler William Dunbar lost nine hundred pounds of opium to theft. *From* The West Shore *magazine.*

A drawing that ran in the *Morning Oregonian* on November 29, 1893, early in the trial of Nat Blum, William Dunbar, Jim Lotan and others. *From left to right*: Judge Bellinger; Lotan employee and fired customs inspector J.T. Coblenz; Dunbar; and Blum. *University of Oregon Libraries.*

more than two tons of opium and running a human-trafficking operation smuggling thousands of undocumented Chinese laborers into Portland.

The trial held the city spellbound. But Lotan and his codefendants hadn't much need to worry. The roster of court officers at this trial reads like an excerpt from the Arlington Club directory, and Lotan was an Arlington Club member.

Lotan himself was represented by future senator Charles W. Fulton. Former and future state Senate president Joseph Simon represented another defendant. The judge was one of Simon's former law partners, and the jury foreman was Lotan's fellow Arlington Club member Charles Ladd—one of Jonathan Bourne's best friends and a good personal friend of Lotan as well.

THE SMUGGLERS GO FREE

The trial ended with a hung jury. The word on the street was that the vote was eleven to one; jury foreman Ladd had refused to vote to convict his friend. A new trial would have to be scheduled.

Meanwhile, Blum, having posted a $1,000 bond, promptly disappeared from the city. The rumor around town was that he had gone east to Washington, D.C., to lobby the president for a pardon. It was difficult for many Portlanders, accustomed though they were to the audacity of this flamboyant smuggler, to believe that he could really be hoping for the president of the United States to issue a pardon to a man whose picture surely appeared next to the word "rapscallion" in Webster's latest dictionary. So most believed that he had skipped on his bail, and as the *Morning Oregonian* put it, "this city shall never see him again."

"It may be remarked right here," the newspaper continued, with sarcasm that still drips fresh and caustic from every syllable 120 years later, "that in case of such a contingency, the people of Portland will try to brokenly live on."

The *Oregonian* went on to remark that the city could never possibly be so fortunate as to never see Blum again because "this is contrary to the tradition in regard to a bad penny."

"In this connection," the newspaper added, "it is but just to say that Blum, whose real name is Blumenkrallowitz, Blumenkrowitz, or something of that sort ending in 'witz' or 'isk,' is no relation to Messrs. Isaac and Leonard Blum, old and well-known residents of this city, who have suffered much annoyance from being asked if they were related to Nat Blum."

Blum did indeed return to Portland and participated in an attempt at a retrial—and then did it again. There were a total of three trials for the accused smugglers from Blum's ring, and the thing dragged on well into 1895 as public and newspaper reporters alike got increasingly tired of the whole thing and as Blum got more and more "creative" in his testimony. A few of the defendants ended up being convicted, but the more Portland saw Nat Blum on the stand, the less credible his testimony became. Lotan never did get convicted.

Dunbar left for China on what he claimed was a business trip and remained there in exile, knowing that he'd be convicted in a trice if he should return. Twenty years later, in November 1913, President Wilson pardoned him, and he was able to finally come home.

Blum eventually drifted away and disappeared. He may have been eliminated by someone—by this time he had plenty of enemies—but he also might very well have simply skipped out on everyone, the police in Portland thinking that he was in federal custody back in Washington and the feds in Washington thinking that he was in Portland. It's hard to say for sure. By the time he disappeared, there was very little interest in his activities, and the newspapers were all sick to death of writing about him.

Without Blum's testimony, Lotan had nothing to fear, but by this time Blum's reputation as an easy liar was so firmly established that it really didn't matter either way.

A few months after the first trial, the impounded *Wilmington* was burned to the waterline and sank in the river, and several months after that, the *Haytian Republic* began its transformation into the SS *Portland*. There is a distinct wistful quality to newspaper coverage of both these events. Wicked and notorious though both ships were, Portlanders were sad to see them go.

ofor.us/wp09

Wicked Politics

It was probably fated that Jonathan Bourne Jr. would get into politics in Oregon. But the path that brought him into politics led straight through the business boardroom.

In 1878, shortly after he landed in Portland, he sent a letter to his brother-in-law, William Abbe, back in New Bedford. After complaining a little about the fact that he lacked a secretary and had to do various chores himself, he added, "I like it though, old man. I can stand it if I only make the money."

And make the money he did. Bourne first finished up his education at Willamette University, taking the bar as a lawyer in 1882. By 1886, he was president of the E.G. Pierce Transfer and Trucking Company, Oregon Milling Company and the Divided Axle Company, as well as a part owner of the township of Grants Pass. He had already started investing in the silver mines in eastern Oregon that would guide so much of his political career to come. And he'd been elected as a state representative the previous year, representing Multnomah County.

At that time, Bourne became a member of the notorious three-man police commission. In this capacity, he would find the resources that would truly make him a force to be reckoned with in Salem—the resources of the "blazing center" of Portland, its North End.

Chief among those resources, of course, was Larry Sullivan. Sullivan ran a polling station near his boardinghouse and occasionally hired his mariner-guests or other wandering hobos to staff it. He'd sit in an upstairs window with a shotgun in his lap, supervising. The transient sailors and

A political cartoon that ran in the *Morning Oregonian* on October 19, 1896, satirizing Jonathan Bourne's support of William Jennings Bryan and the "Free Silver" populist movement. Bourne, a Republican, got criticized vigorously by the *Oregonian* for this "betrayal." *University of Oregon Libraries.*

rootless vagabonds would cram it full of ballots and disappear back into the timberlands or over the sea.

Bourne was a Republican, but that didn't exactly mean what it means today. Partisan politics in late 1800s Portland, and in Oregon generally, were very different.

First, the state was overwhelmingly Republican at the time. So most of the time, while the junior Democratic Party struggled to be as relevant as it could, the real struggle was among two rival factions of the Republican Party.

The old-guard conservative Republicans had several huge advantages in that their number included Harvey Scott, the fearsome editor of the *Morning Oregonian*, as well as the overwhelming majority of the controllers of wealth, both inside and outside the state.

Opposing them were the "silver Republicans," a more populist group that developed into the progressive Republicans of the type made famous by Bourne's later political idol, Theodore Roosevelt. This group was far more eclectic and independent and had little use for "party discipline." It, too, had a mouthpiece in the feisty but far less influential *Portland Evening Telegram*. This, of course, was Bourne's group.

Bourne's fortunes continued to wax, both financially and politically. He was always a little unpredictable, and he was forever applying the considerable force of his creativity in devious and audacious ways. He bought votes, plied legislators with liquor and collaborated with Sullivan to make the North End into a well-oiled machine dedicated to voter fraud.

In the election of 1896, though, Bourne really managed to outdo himself, as well as to win for himself and for Oregon a reputation for hard-core political chicanery and unabashed debauchery that wouldn't fade for decades to come. It would cast a shadow over his future political career, and it would earn for him the implacable and eternal enmity of the formidable Harvey Scott.

But it would be so worth it.

THE HOLD-UP SESSION

The election of 1896 in Oregon was like a black-comedy routine. By now, Bourne owned a big string of silver mines in eastern Oregon and the Idaho Territory, and he even had a booming Blue Mountain mining town named after him. His great political passion was for "bi-metallism," or the backing of U.S. currency with silver as well as gold—because, of course, it was good for the silver business. Bourne therefore was pushing hard for the election of Democrat William Jennings Bryan, the "Free Silver Candidate," even though he himself was a Republican. He was also campaigning hard among the returning legislators for his friend and fellow Free Silver Republican John H. Mitchell to be returned to the U.S. Senate; at that time, senators were appointed by state legislatures and not directly elected by voters.

In an effort to deliver the state's electoral college votes to Bryan, Bourne and his fellow deep-pocketed cronies hired a friend of Larry Sullivan's named Billy Smith, a wanted criminal from California who, for a fee, would bring a large group of trained and disciplined serial voters up from the Golden State on election day, stuff ballot boxes all over Portland and disappear the following day like one of Mary Cook's smoke rings on the wind.

It was to be a team effort: Billy and Larry would stuff ballot boxes all over town until they burst, helping Bryan and Bourne win the popular vote; meanwhile, Bourne, armed with $225,000 in Southern Pacific Railroad money, would be making the rounds of the legislators, schmoozing and exchanging stacks of cash for signed pledges to support Mitchell. Mitchell, after being elected, would then call in as many markers as necessary to elevate Bourne to the job of Speaker of the House. It would be as beautiful and artful a work of choreographed political debauchery as ever graced the Beaver State.

Senator John Mitchell as he looked in the 1870s. *J. Gaston*, Portland: Its History and Builders *(1911)*.

Billy and Larry did a yeoman's job all over Portland that November, cramming every ballot box with thousands of bogus votes for Bryan for president and for Bourne for the Oregon State House of Representatives.

The results were mixed. In Portland, Bourne easily won

the seat he sought and easily secured enough pledges of support to guarantee Mitchell's return to the Senate. It looked like he was about to be Speaker.

The campaign for Bryan was not as successful, but not for the reason you might think. "The reason they didn't win was that [Henry] Corbett employed more men and sent them up and down the river to vote, and they voted at outside towns as well as in Portland," wrote Cordelia M. Pierce (later Oregon governor Walter Pierce's wife) in her diary.

But Bourne couldn't have been very upset about that. Bryan lost to McKinley by a margin far too big for Oregon's votes to have changed anything. The important thing was that Bourne was in the House. And as soon as the legislators were seated, one of the first orders of business would be voting to reappoint Mitchell, and after that—hello, speakership!

After the election, though, Bourne started hearing some disturbing rumors. The word was that Mitchell, after securing his reelection with Bourne's help, planned to renege on their deal just as soon as he got back to Washington. Not the speakership part of the deal—the free-silver part, which was far more important to Bourne.

Bourne was not a man to sit around and hope for the best when a rumor like that is on the wind. He asked Mitchell flat out, the next time he saw him, what his intentions were. This is how he described the ensuing conversation to his friend and legislative colleague Walter Pierce:

> *After the November election, 1896, I met Sen. Mitchell on the streets in Portland. I said to him, "Senator, the report here in Portland is, and at the [Arlington] Club, that when you are reelected senator in this upcoming legislature, you expect to go back to Washington, join Mark Hanna and the gold crowd, going completely back on your silver friends. I don't believe a word of it. You won't go back on me?"*
>
> *He hesitated. I said, "Out with it: Tell me the fact." The senator said, "That is what I am going to do, Jonathan."*

It was a serious double cross, and both men knew it. But elder statesman Mitchell must have been a bit taken aback by the relatively youthful Bourne's reaction:

> *I looked him straight in the face and I said, "You are not going to be elected by this legislative body that meets next January." The Senator replied, "Jonathan, you can't [stop me]. You took the pledges from the men who were candidates when you gave them the money…and you took those pledges*

to the Southern Pacific Railroad which put up the $225,000 that you distributed among candidates for the legislature. Those pledges have been signed. They are locked up in the Southern Pacific Railroad safe…You can't help it. I will be elected."

"I don't know how it is going to be prevented, but you are not going to be elected," I said.

Bourne's Scheme

Bourne knew that Mitchell was right about one thing: there was nothing he would be able to do to change the way the vote would go when the subject of Mitchell's reelection came up. Odd though it sounds to the modern ear, the politicos who signed those pledges at Bourne's urging considered that to be their word of honor as gentlemen, even though in signing them they had been violating several federal laws and essentially swindling their constituents. Regardless of Mitchell's betrayal, they would vote for him. In 1890s Portland, and in Oregon as a whole, the most respected politician was not the man who could not be bought—it was the man who, once bought, would stay bought in the face of temptation to renege.

However, Bourne mused, what if the subject never came up? If the legislature failed to elect anyone in time for inauguration day, the governor was supposed to appoint somebody. And the governor who'd just been elected—Republican William P. Lord—was a friend of Bourne's. All Bourne had to do was figure out how to prevent the legislature from voting until inauguration day. How might he do that?

A few days later, a curious article appeared in the *Portland Morning Oregonian*, which, like everyone else in the world, still thought that Bourne and Mitchell had a rock-solid alliance.

MR. BOURNE'S FIGHT: SENATOR MITCHELL WILL
HELP HIM TO BE SPEAKER

---

*Being Assured of Desired Support, He Renews His Campaign
with Great Energy*

The engagement by Mr. Jonathan Bourne of 19 rooms in the Eldridge Block, Salem, as well as the lease of the handsome Keller House, on State Street, has created uncommon interest in political circles in this city…It would appear that he is entering upon the fight [for the speakership] *with a degree of ostentation unusual in speakership contests, and it is not easy to see on the surface why quarters so extensive should have been engaged. The real reason probably is that the Eldridge Block rooms will be used during the season as supplementary Mitchell headquarters.*

Given Mitchell's track record as an experienced politician, it's safe to guess that he read that article with mounting alarm, knowing, as no one else in the world did at the time, that Bourne was no longer even thinking about the speakership. What could he be up to, he must have wondered?

A few days later, he learned. Everyone learned.

The mustachioed marauder went into action with classic Bourne flair. First, he reached out across the aisle to an earnest Populist legislator, William U'Ren, who must have been very surprised indeed; days before, Bourne had been his number-two political enemy, right behind Mitchell.

Together, the two strange new bedfellows formulated a plan. U'Ren, when the legislature convened, would coordinate parliamentary delaying tactics from the inside. As for Bourne, his role in the plot would be rather more unconventional.

Bourne set his plan in motion just before the legislature was to convene by gathering together about $80,000—including $10,000 skimmed from the operations of his North End friends' waterfront gambling joints, opium dens, brothels and shanghai boardinghouses. He then used the cash, and those nineteen rooms the *Oregonian* was so puzzled about, to throw a massive, six-week-long drunken party for his fellow legislators.

FORTY DAYS OF "BOURNE'S HAREM"

The party would rage for forty days, in an apparently unintentional parody of the Biblical account of Jesus's time of temptation in the wilderness.

"I…hired the best chef in the state of Oregon; sent him to Salem to fix up apartments in the Eldridge Block; things to eat and drink and entertainment," Bourne later recalled. "I said to the chef, 'I pay all expenses. I want to take care of all my friends in the lower House who signed pledges with me, the friends of silver.'"

That chef certainly didn't come from Bourne's North End, but some of the "entertainment" might have. The Eldridge Block quickly developed some colorful new nicknames. "Bourne's Harem" was one; "the Den of Prostitution and Evil" was another. State senator George C. Brownell of Oregon City wrote disapprovingly that legislators at Bourne's party "were kept drunk and intoxicated for days."

This was the forty-day debauch that was to go down in song and legend as "the hold-up session."

Now, keep in mind that these disparaging monikers and negative comments all came from people who were not invited to this party—who were not Bourne's "friends of silver." They may have had personal rather than factual reasons to suggest that Bourne was plying the "friends of silver" with the favors of friendly ladies from the old North End. But still, given Bourne's style and connections in Portland, they may very well have been true. Indeed, it would be a little disappointing if they were not.

Also, at that time, the legislature as a whole had a really terrible reputation for exactly that sort of thing. "Oregon enjoyed the unenviable reputation of having one of the most corrupt and inefficient governments to be found north of Mexico and west of Pennsylvania," wrote historian Cecil T. Thompson in 1927. "As soon as the Legislature convened, a troupe of prostitutes quite regularly convened at Salem—the lawmakers, in some cases, attaching them to the state payroll. Drunkenness and debauchery commonly prevailed throughout the whole legislative session." So if Bourne was in fact operating a harem, he wasn't exactly breaking new ground.

Whether prostitution was involved or not, the purpose of Bourne's party was to prevent the House from being convened. So long as the House did not convene, remaining members could not vote to vacate their seats or send the police out after them. And so long as enough legislators were unfit for duty—that is, intoxicated—at any given time, no quorum could be assembled anyway.

SUCCESS!...WELL, SORT OF

By inauguration day, nothing had come out of the state House at all, on Mitchell's reelection or any other topic. A quorum of legislators had not even been sworn in. The remaining Mitchell-friendly legislators tried to organize a rump session, but it lacked any legal standing. The Senate, which was led by Bourne's old friend and ally Joseph Simon, was of no help at all to Mitchell's friends. So, as Bourne had planned, Governor Lord was forced to make an emergency appointment, and he named Henry Corbett to Mitchell's Senate seat. Yes, that's right, the same Henry Corbett who had outfoxed Bourne in the ballot-stuffing contest the previous year, now a fast and firm ally.

Corbett was delighted, of course. He had long cherished hopes of being sent to the Senate. Alas, when he arrived in Washington, he met a chilly reception. Stories of the hold-up session had preceded him, and Capitol Hill was atwitter with them. Execs at the Southern Pacific Railroad, which had "invested" 225 bills on the project to get Mitchell elected, were furious and pulled every string they could get their hands on. Possibly as a result, the U.S. Senate refused to seat Corbett.

A crestfallen Corbett had to return to Portland, and Oregon's second Senate seat remained vacant for two full years. Finally, in late 1898, a special session of the legislature elected Joseph Simon—Bourne's friend from the state Senate—to Mitchell's seat.

Mitchell was done for, at least for the time being. Bourne had won, and in the process he had earned for Oregon a reputation for political chicanery and wide-open public vice that wouldn't fade for decades to come.

BOURNE'S MIDLIFE CRISIS

It was just a few years after this dark triumph that Bourne, the legendary debauched "machine man" of Portland politics, did something that shocked everyone: he became a reformer.

There was one more dirty election for a U.S. senator, taking place in 1900, and it was a rematch: Bourne was again trying to deny Mitchell the nomination and get Corbett the job. George C. Brownell, writing about the incident ten years later, recalled that Bourne "bought men and paid them in money and whisky and other things for their votes." (Brownell, no friend of Bourne, likely meant "other things" to refer to exactly what you think. And he may very well have been right.) Historian E. Kimbark MacColl reported that "one House member, a parishioner of a leading Portland church, was allegedly given $100 every time he voted for Corbett, plus a slug of whisky in the cloakroom."

Again, though, the Southern Pacific outspent him, and Bourne blamed "four traitors" who had been induced by the torrent of railroad payoffs to change their votes. Again, Bourne was left with his purse considerably lightened and with no soap to show for it. And—what was probably worse for a man like Bourne—Mitchell had the last laugh on him.

At this point, Bourne, the consummate corrupt politician, the man with the connections to get anybody anything, seems to have had a sort of epiphany. It may have grown out of a burning determination to finally outfox Mitchell one way or the other—but if so, it's clear that it quickly turned into something deeper, more important and nobler than a simple political revenge play.

In the 1870s, you'll remember, Bourne had come to Portland as a twentysomething libertine with nearly unlimited income, dropping into the North End like a cocked pistol and spending twenty-five years there having the time of his life. But by 1900, he was forty-five years old—still relatively young, but old enough to think about it.

By now, it was perfectly clear that he was never going to be able to raise enough money from his own personal resources and from his friends in the North End to compete with people who controlled the profits of companies with nationwide monopolies. If they wanted John Mitchell appointed as a senator so that he could facilitate their land grabs, they would spend what it took to do that. Bourne was playing a sucker's game, and he was wasting his money.

So he once again joined forces with William U'Ren to form an organization called the People's Power League, under U'Ren's leadership. The plan was to get voter approval of the Oregon voter initiative and referendum system and to make U.S. senators be elected by the people and not the legislature.

Together, U'Ren and Bourne succeeded in that quest, to the great dismay and fury of Oregon's dominant political establishment. And Jonathan Bourne, who could have taught seminars on "how to make political corruption work for you," became an indispensable part of stopping it.

In the years after this coup, the conventional wisdom of both the right and the left has been that Bourne did this as a cynical ploy to advance his political career. "He is not a Republican," sneered Harvey Scott, articulating the conservative establishment's view in the editorial columns of the *Morning Oregonian* in 1914, after Bourne had been defeated for reelection to the U.S. Senate. "He is essentially a political freebooter, who practices allegiance to no party and who is concerned about the fortunes of no candidacy but his own."

It's a telling piece of editorial work—not least because of its timing, coming out as it did in "kick 'em when they're down" fashion after Bourne had already been defeated. But it articulates the Republican establishment's opinion of Bourne as well as anything. They were not about to forgive him for his betrayal in making common cause with U'Ren and, essentially, cutting off their ability to loot the political system.

The liberal progressives weren't overly fond of him either and tended to agree with Scott's assessment. Uncomfortable sharing the credit for one of the most spectacular populist triumphs of the age, they spun Bourne as a dupe, a tool they'd been able to manipulate and play off against the plutocratic establishment to achieve their political goals. In Lincoln Steffens's unsubtle and fawning article in *The American* magazine, "U'Ren the Lawgiver," Bourne is presented as a schemer whose single-minded focus on the speakership makes him easily manipulated into a weapon for U'Ren to use against Mitchell, and his role in the successful establishment of the initiative and referendum system is reduced to a grudging mention of "support."

Historian Pike, in his dissertation, argues convincingly that the conventional wisdom of both right and left was simply wrong:

> *Bourne was often accused of political opportunism, of self-interest, and of an overwhelming desire for publicity. Looking at his career as a whole, we can see that these charges are not well-founded. Least valid of all are the charges of opportunism and self-interest. If they were at all true he would not have been found so often in opposition to the dominant political forces: the Taft Administration, the regular Republican organization of his own state, and the Wilson administration. If he had "gone along," his Senatorial career probably would have lasted longer than one term.*

There is, of course, another theory that would account for Bourne's sudden change, and it goes like this. Here's this wayward youth, exiled from his home, who settles in on the farthest frontier. He spends two decades playing at politics and business as if nothing really mattered, until suddenly he encounters the rivers of cash coming from the other side of the country from railroad monopolies and timber empires with unlimited funds...and with no regard whatever for his new home. He realizes that the backroom slug-of-whiskey systems that he's had so much fun with are freely available to those who not only oppose him but are also ready and willing and able to turn what has become his new home into a banana republic, in which (as he sees it) responsible business leaders who actually live in the community have no real voice in how it's governed. And he's forty-five years old—old enough to know better, old enough to be thinking like a man going through a midlife crisis.

He has a choice to make. Will he be an increasingly irrelevant part of the problem, reaching out to grab his share of the spoils and ending his life in a splendid mansion in a ruined land, surrounded by tainted riches? Or will he reach across party lines, sacrifice his opportunities for personal enrichment and do something that he can be proud of in his sunset years?

Maybe this aging hell-raiser looked at what was going on and, with his mind focused by a bruising and impoverishing battle that put an unpopular, corrupt and utterly amoral man into the Oregon Senate, thought, "I'm going to stop this."

Maybe. It's worth bearing in mind here that Bourne's idol, Theodore Roosevelt, already had a track record of reacting in exactly that way to situations of this sort. Whatever the reason, in the early 1900s, Bourne was pushing for direct citizen involvement, a goal that would make the kind of brazen corruption that had characterized the 1890s unthinkable—and he got it.

He became the first Oregon senator ever elected by a popular vote. Once in office, he worked diligently and soberly on a long list of boring but important accomplishments—the Parcel Post system was his biggest achievement—and then lost his bid for a second term in a Republican primary.

By the time of his death in 1940, Bourne had become respected as an elder statesman in the same sort of grudging way President Richard Nixon was in his later years. But unlike Nixon, few actually remembered much about his career—about either the important parts that came late in his run or the interesting parts from earlier.

However, it's probably safe to say that if he'd stayed in Massachusetts, Oregon would have become a very different place—and probably not a better one, either.

ofor.us/wp10

The End of the Golden Age

The last few years of the nineteenth century were really the high-water mark of corruption, vice and sin in Portland. After that, as the town eased into the new century under the sober leadership of reform-minded mayor Harry Lane after 1900, it was still plenty sinful, vice-riddled and corrupt, but those waters were receding. And that was for several reasons.

There was, of course, the Bourne-U'Ren political alliance, which was itself a reaction to the unsustainability of the old Gilded Age political system.

Another important reason was the coming Lewis and Clark Centennial Exposition, slated for 1905. Portland was the smallest city to have ever hosted one of these national expositions. Planning for it got underway in 1901, and soon Portlanders started realizing that visitors would be arriving in their city on the train, and if something wasn't done, they'd be passing windows full of welcoming prostitutes, rowdy saloons, gambling joints, opium dens and drunken sailors as they arrived at the Union Station. Suddenly the appearance and reputation of the city was on everyone's mind, and Portland had found the political will to do something about it.

But the biggest change may well have been in technology. The 1890s were the heyday of the gangs of bachelor laborers that fueled the wild and lusty round-the-clock debauchery in the North End. In the early 1900s, those bachelor gigs were starting to change in ways that would make things better for just about everyone.

A "Photochrom" color lithograph of the view of Portland as seen from Council Crest in 1901. *Library of Congress.*

Better steam donkey engines and narrow-gauge railroads were making life less difficult and isolated for the crews of loggers working in the woods. Most of them were still ready to do some serious hell-roaring when they got into town, but some of them were starting to actually get married and have kids. This was easier to do once it became possible to stay in the woods for only a week or two rather than for several months at a time—and maybe even come home on the weekends.

As for the miners, well, the bottom dropped right out from under them in the early 1900s. A cadre of sharp-elbowed fast-talkers had figured out that hordes of suckers back east were just itching to invest in mining operations in the West. These characters set up dummy mines or bought up old played-out operations, salted them with gold and used them to put on a show in order to fleece the investors who were buying stock.

The most egregious example of this was a hard-rock mining boomtown in eastern Oregon named after Jonathan Bourne himself—Bourne, Oregon, population roughly 1,500 at the time; it's a ghost town today. A character named F. Wallace White moved into the town of Bourne, bought a bunch of played-out gold and silver mines and started using the town as a stage from which to put on a show for suckers back east.

The Wild and Lusty Underworld of a Frontier Seaport Town

Downtown businesspeople at the corner of Third and Washington Streets during the flood of 1894. *Portland City Archives.*

When those suckers finally got wise, the word went around that Oregon gold and silver mines were scams. The governor of Pennsylvania at one time actually tried to make the sale of stock in any Oregon gold mine illegal in his state—a step that, as it turned out, was completely unnecessary because by then the word was out. Capital flow all but stopped for gold mines both crooked and honest. The eastern Oregon mining industry faded away in all but one or two especially rich spots. Hard-rock miners, once a common sight on Skid Road, became rare; many of them became homesteaders and settled down.

And then, of course, there were the sailors, for years the lowest caste of laborers on the waterfront. But their position was changing too.

For at least a dozen years, steam engines and drive systems had been steadily getting more efficient, and by the turn of the century, there was no longer any economic reason to build a windjammer instead of a steamer. And there was no comparison between the difficulty faced by a windjammer sailor and a steamer crewman. Not only that, since they weren't dependent on the weather and didn't need all that weather-catching rigging high overhead, steamers were far less dangerous to sail on. Ship owners might pay a little more to get across the ocean with one, but they made up for the expense very quickly with savings in insurance premiums and labor costs. It took far fewer men to run a steamer.

A panoramic lithograph of Portland published in 1888 as a fold-out in *The West Shore* magazine. *Library of Congress.*

As mentioned earlier, the combination of better working conditions and less demand for men took the business right out from under the sailors' boardinghouses (the crimps). Remember, these guys were in business specifically to enable the sailing ships' owners to pay less than the fair market value of the labor they were buying, by forcing those unfortunate enough to have fallen into the business to continue shipping out when they would much rather have been doing something else. When the job they were supplying labor for suddenly became attractive to the job-seeking world at large, there was no reason for ships' masters to deal with the crimps at all, and increasingly, they didn't.

Merchant mariners, like the loggers, started being able to settle down and have families. This took a lot of the edge off their in-port carousing, and businesses that catered to them—like Liverpool Liz and her Senate Saloon—started to fade.

It wasn't that everything started getting better all at once, of course. There were still plenty of tall ships plying the oceans, operated by people who either couldn't afford to replace them or were too tradition-minded to do so. Shipyards were still building barques in the 1920s, just not very many

of them. There was still a demand for deep-water sailors on wind-powered ships, but only the most ignorant, incompetent and desperate sailors would ship out on one; anyone who had a choice shipped on a steamer. So for a few years, shanghaiing actually got worse rather than better.

But by the outbreak of World War I, Portland's hell-roaring golden age was mostly a memory, and Skid Road was a shadow of its former self. It was still formidable, especially when the loggers blew in, but it wasn't like it had once been.

Ah, the good old days. Aren't you glad they're gone?

Source Notes

CHAPTER 1

The secondary sources of greatest general usefulness were E. Kimbark MacColl's *Merchants, Money and Power 1843–1913* (Portland, OR: Georgian Press, 1988) and Jewel Lansing's *Portland: People, Politics and Power* (Corvallis: Oregon State University Press, 2003), as well as a number of retrospective newspaper articles by Stewart Holbrook, published in the *Portland Oregonian* in 1936 (in the Sunday magazine supplement) and 1959 (in the Oregon Sesquicentennial supplement).

The description of Portland's New England elite, midwestern middle class and North End transients came from "Portland: A Pilgrim's Progress," by Dean Collins, published in editor Duncan Aikman's *Taming of the Frontier* (New York: Minton, 1925).

CHAPTER 2

Information about Jonathan Bourne's early years came from articles in the *Portland Morning Oregonian* and Albert Heisey Pike Jr.'s "Jonathan Bourne Jr., Progressive" (PhD dissertation, University of Oregon, 1957), along with MacColl's book.

Chapter 3

The main primary source for this chapter is *Edward Chambreau: His Autobiography*, collected and annotated in a PhD dissertation by Timothy Lee Wehrkamp (University of Oregon) in 1976. It is the main source for the details of Chambreau's story, along with the details of how "blackleg" gamblers and saloonkeepers operated and how they collaborated with corrupt cops.

Information about the prevalence and techniques of cheating at the game of faro also came from John N. Maskelyne's *Sharps and Flats: A Complete Revelation of the Secrets of Cheating* (New York: Logmans, 1894).

MacColl's *Merchants, Money and Power* was useful in this chapter as well, primarily for details of James Lappeus's career in public service, and Paul Gilman Merriam's "Portland, Oregon, 1840–1890: A Social and Economic History" (PhD dissertation, University of Oregon, 1971), was a great source of details about, among other things, the Oro Fino Theatre.

The story of young J.P. Cochran was told in the *Portland Evening Telegram*, a short item on page 2 in the December 9, 1892 edition and a longer one on page 1 of December 15. The *Telegram* of this era has the best rabble-rousing, scandal-mongering racy prose of any paper in the city.

The statistics on licensed drinking establishments came out of Malcolm Clark Jr.'s *Oregon Historical Quarterly* article, "The War on the Webfoot Saloon" (March 1957).

Chapter 4

Information on the great moral crusade came from the *Morning Oregonian*, April 10, 1895, as well as August 2 and 9 of 1936, in which Stewart Holbrook's serialized article appears.

For Mary Cook, see Stewart Holbrook's article on "The Three Sirens of Portland," as told to him by Spider Johnson, published in the *American Mercury* in May 1948.

For Liverpool Liz, see Holbrook's "Three Sirens" again but also the *Portland Oregonian*, March 8, 15 and 22, 1936 (Holbrook's article on Fred Merrill).

For the story of Boneyard Mary, see the *Morning Oregonian*, February 25 and 26, 1878. The information that's between the lines of these two stories is fascinating.

For Nancy Boggs, see Holbrook again. He wrote two different versions of this same story. The more credible of the two is in *Holy Old Mackinaw*

(New York: Macmillan, 1938), and the less, in "Three Sirens." Both are clearly folkloric to some degree; they're the reminiscences of a colorful character over beers in a slightly dangerous dive in the late 1920s. However, the two accounts don't match up. One says that Nancy's brothel-boat was anchored in the very same spot in the river the next morning, as if nothing had happened; the other says it ended up anchored a little downriver at Linnton, out of both Portlands' jurisdiction. The "same-spot" story was first published in the *American Mercury*, and I suspect that the confusion was introduced by an overambitious editor and that the closest to the real story is the Linnton variant.

The vice crusade of '96 came from a Stewart Holbrook article published July 26, 1936, and one by Herbert Lundy, April 2, 1939, both in the *Portland Oregonian*; and an *Evening Telegram* piece run on December 5, 1892.

CHAPTER 5

The story of Aquilla Ernest Clark is related in Richard Dillon's *Shanghaiing Days* (New York: Coward, 1961), which is a source of many other tidbits in this chapter, including the life of a shanghaied sailor, details of the West Coast crimping scene, how the crimping business worked in general, the trouble ship captains had with Sullivan's consortium of crimps and the story of Andy Furuseth. Dillon's book is in part a work of journalism, as he was able to interview a number of people who had been directly involved in the crimping business.

By the way, the captain and officers of the *T.F. Oakes*—the ship Clark was shanghaied onto—were charged with cruelty on several occasions, including one incident in 1895 in which a man dying of stomach cancer and burning with fever was forced to work on deck until he dropped dead and a notorious 1897 voyage in which the sailors arrived in port nearly starved to death. In 1897, the *Morning Oregonian* noted that the "T.F. Oakes never yet made port without a complaint of either cruelty or starvation coming from the forecastle [the sailors' quarters]."

The story of Bunco Kelly came from Stewart Holbrook's "Bunco Kelly, King of the Crimps" (*American Mercury*, October 1948), along with articles in the *Portland Evening Telegram*, *Daily Astorian* and *Portland Morning Oregonian*. Portland historian James Terence Fisher has also tried to confirm the details of the *Flying Prince* incident, without success.

Some information on Kelly also came from Joseph "Bunco" Kelly's own autobiography, *Thirteen Years in the Oregon Penitentiary* (published with no publisher's name on it in 1908; free PDF version available through Google Books).

The life of a logger in a timber camp, compared with that of a deep-water sailor, came from Holbrook's *Holy Old Mackinaw*, another somewhat journalistic work based on Holbrook's own career working in such a camp in the 1920s, and from Basil Lubbock's *The Last of the Windjammers*, vol. 1 (New York: Brown, 1927). Another source was Carol Lind's *Big Timber Big Men: A History of Loggers in a New Land* (Seattle, WA: Hancock, 1978), which, while largely sourced from Holbrook, includes some additional useful details.

CHAPTER 6

Historian and former Portland city auditor Jewel Lansing, in *Portland: People, Politics and Power* (Corvallis: Oregon State University Press, 2003), gives the best methodical account of the growth of Portland city government that I've found. Her book is the primary source for nuts-and-bolts details of how the city marshal's office and police department evolved.

Another vital secondary source was the Portland Police Department's millennium yearbook, titled *Portland's Finest, Past and Present* (Paducah, KY: Turner, 2000); it has no listed author.

The Danford Balch case is covered in E. Kimbark MacColl's *Merchants, Money and Power* (Portland, OR: Georgian, 1988), but a more thorough and, it must be said, entertaining treatment of the Balch case can be found in Doug Kenck-Crispin and Andy Lindberg's "Kick Ass Oregon History" podcast (2011) at www.orhistory.com. As the title suggests, this source might not be safe for work; both Lindberg and Kenck-Crispin present the material in a highly vernacular manner, dropping the occasional f-bomb along the way.

The story of reform-minded mayor Mason and his attempts to get the city's vice under control is also from MacColl.

CHAPTER 7

The stories of all these mayors can be found in E. Kimbark MacColl's and Jewel Lansing's books. Pennoyer's story came from these sources, as well as from John B. Horner's *Oregon: Her History, Her Great Men, Her Literature* (Corvallis, OR: *Gazette-Times*, 1919) and Dick Pintarch's article "His Eccentricity: Gov. Sylvester Pennoyer," from *Oregon* magazine, reprinted in *Great Moments in Oregon History* (Portland: New Oregon, 1987).

CHAPTER 8

This chapter was primarily sourced from contemporary accounts in the *Portland Evening Telegram*, which appeared almost daily, usually on page 1, from November 22 through December 23, 1893; the *Portland Oregonian*, 1893–95; and the *New York Times*, July 25, 1893. The *Telegram*'s coverage of the trial was far better than the *Oregonian*'s, most likely because defendant James Lotan was a friend and political associate of *Oregonian* editor Harvey Scott.

Information about the discovery of the SS *Portland*, née SS *Haytian Republic*, was from the *Juneau Empire*, September 9, 2004.

Portland City Directories for 1892–95 were the sources for the various businesses and their locations.

Details of the Haitian blockade runners are from John O'Brien and Horace H. Smith's *A Captain Unafraid: The Strange Adventures of Dynamite Johnny O'Brien* (New York: Harper, 1912).

CHAPTER 9

Biographical information about Jonathan Bourne Jr. came from Albert Heisey Pike Jr.'s PhD dissertation and from *Oregon Cattleman/Governor/Congressman*, the memoirs of former governor Walter Pierce (Portland: Oregon Historical Society Press, 1981), as well as MacColl and Lansing.

Contemporary newspaper sources included the *Portland Morning Oregonian* from January 6 through February 19, 1897, and October 5, 1954.

More information about the debauchery of 1890s legislatures came from Cecil T. Thompson's "The Origins of Direct Legislation in Oregon" (master's thesis, University of Oregon, 1927).

Lincoln Steffens's article in *The American* magazine, "U'Ren the Lawgiver" (1908), was useful chiefly as an articulation of the progressive left's attitude toward Bourne. A classic "puff piece," it is provably counterfactual in several places, omits uncomfortable parts of U'Ren's story (such as his estrangement from the Lewelling family) and shows every sign of having been crafted with a personal and political agenda in mind.

CHAPTER 10

Information about the town of Bourne, F. Wallace White and Oregon's fading hard-rock mining industry came from Miles F. Potter's *Oregon's Golden Years: Bonanza of the West* (Caldwell, ID: Caxton, 1982) and Stewart Holbrook's *The Far Corner* (New York: Macmillan, 1952).

Information about the changing of logging technology is from Stewart Holbrook's *Holy Old Mackinaw*.

The information about the changing life of a sailor, and the effect that had on the remaining windjammer fleet, is from Basil Lubbock's *The Last of the Windjammers* and James Gibbs's *Shipwrecks of the Pacific Coast* (Portland, OR: Binford, 1957).

ofor.us/wpau

About the Author

Finn J.D. John (finnjohn.com or @ offbeatoregon on Twitter) is from Oregon's north Willamette Valley and is a graduate of Central Catholic High School in southeast Portland. Since 2008, Finn, a longtime newspaper reporter and editor, has produced a weekly syndicated column titled "Offbeat Oregon History," which is published in thirteen different Oregon community newspapers around the state.

Finn teaches new media communications at Oregon State University and is a public historian by avocation. He maintains a website at www. offbeatoregon.com as both a public history resource and a laboratory in which to experiment with trans-media franchise building and social media tools. Currently the "Offbeat Oregon" franchise includes a daily RSS news feed and iTunes podcast feed optimized for smartphone use, an active Facebook page and a Twitter feed; future plans include an Instagram account and a YouTube channel.

He is currently working on a narrative nonfiction book about ex-president and former Oregonian Herbert Hoover, who, before becoming the most hated president of the twentieth century, saved the entire nation of Belgium from starving to death during World War II.

Finn lives near Albany with his wife, Natalie, and son, Nathaniel.

Visit us at
www.historypress.net

ofor.us/wphp